Rock & Roll's
Most Wanted

Rock & Roll's Most Wanted

The Top 10 Book of Lame Lyrics,
Egregious Egos, and Other
Oddities

Stuart Shea

Brassey's, Inc.

WASHINGTON, D.C.

**Library of Congress Cataloging-in-Publication
Data**

Shea, Stuart.
    Rock & roll's most wanted : the top 10
book of lame lyrics, egregious egos, and
other oddities, / Stuart Shea.—1st ed.
        p.   cm.
Includes index.
    ISBN 1-57488-477-8 (pbk.)
    1. Rock music—Humor. 2. Rock music—
History and criticism. I. Title: Rock and
roll's most wanted II. Title

    ML3534.S475 2002
    781.66—dc21

                                    2002002658

Printed in Canada.

Brassey's, Inc.
22841 Quicksilver Drive
Dulles, Virginia 20166

Designed by Pen & Palette Unlimited.

First Edition
10 9 8 7 6 5 4 3 2 1

Dedication

To John Lennon, Buddy Holly, Otis Redding, Nick Drake, Billie Holiday, Sandy Denny, and all musicians, living and dead: the world moves because of you.

Contents

Photographs

Preface

April 6, 1974: I remember it as if it were just last month. It's the day I bought my first rock & roll record.

It was only a few months earlier that I first realized people could actually *own* the music played by the local Top 40 radio stations, Chicago's legendary WLS ("The Rock of Chicago") and "Super" WCFL.

One day, a friend brought a few 45 RPM records to school to play for someone's birthday party. I was just about to turn 11 and, on that day, I discovered that anyone could buy popular music.

Although I grew up with my mom, dad, and two brothers in a musical environment, most of our records were either classical discs or kids' songs. The only pop music in the house was on the two Beatles albums my dad had picked up in the late

'60s. We loved these albums, but thought they were singular in the universe—that there was no other music made comparable to *Revolver* and *Sgt. Pepper's Lonely Hearts Club Band.* (Actually, in a way, I still believe that.)

So when my mom idly mentioned that maybe we could all go downtown and shop for records on some Saturday, I leapt at the opportunity.

The next Saturday, my mom, my younger brothers, John and Tom, and I took the #203 bus into downtown Evanston. We three kids were full of anticipation. Stepping into Laury's Records (R.I.P.) for the first time, we were agog.

While looking at the WCFL survey of the Top 40 records in the city, we were informed that all of them were available—and that we could each buy *two!*

While it doesn't necessarily fill me with pride to say that the first record I ever bought was sung by Carly Simon, her duet with James Taylor, "Mockingbird," was one of my favorites at the time. That, and Elton John's "Bennie and the Jets" were my selections.

My brothers picked four other current hit records: Blue Swede's "Hooked on a Feeling," Jim Stafford's "Spiders and Snakes," "Jet" by Paul McCartney & Wings, and "Seasons in the Sun" by Terry Jacks.

While not all of these songs have stood the test of time, I have warm memories of them, like those engendered by a first kiss or by a long-ago birthday party when your mother baked your favorite cake.

And when I think of those records, I am frozen in time as an 11-year-old boy, wide open to the possibilities of the world, unknowingly about to jump headlong into a lifelong love affair with music.

Music can take away your troubles, or it can express them. It can anchor you to the world, reminding you of what is important and real, or it can transport you, like all the best art does, into a magical make-believe world where everything is valid and you are accepted for who you are.

One way I can express my love for music is to write about it, to collect stories, to honor the musicians who have made it. That's what I've tried to do with this book, digging old stories up, reexpressing forgotten ideas, and bringing seemingly unrelated characteristics together into groups.

Even those records my brothers and I were able to purchase on April 6, 1974, have stories and interesting facts attached to them.

For instance? Well, Carly Simon and James Taylor were one of the only married couples to have a hit record. Blue Swede didn't speak English.

"Seasons in the Sun" was one of a whole flock of death songs that spread over the airwaves in 1974–75. Paul McCartney recorded "Jet" in Nigeria, at a studio owned by former Cream drummer Ginger Baker.

After I moved on from my early days of AM radio, there would be more stories, more music, more worlds to discover. With the encouragement and help of friends, I worked backward to '50s and '60s rock and R&B, then, in the late '70s, I picked up on punk, ska (the Jamaican precursor to reggae), and new wave. Next I was led to British post-punk, American indie rock, Western swing, experimental composition, techno, ambient sound, Latin rhythms of all sorts, and house. I've been truly enriched by all the music I've heard.

And in that ecumenical spirit, I refer in this book to music that may barely skirt the rock genre as "rock & roll." That means there is room here for the Beatles, Stones, the Jefferson Airplane, and Camper Van Beethoven, but also for Sonny and Cher, R. Kelly, Tammi Terrell, and William Orbit. Loosely defined, it is music aimed at the Top 40 charts and mostly bought by teenagers and young adults.

In a way, that ecumenical spirit of '70s pop-rock radio helped forge my tastes, and that's why I wanted to do this book—to share my love for rock & roll music, the music that, as John Sebastian wrote, "can set you free." And to share my love for the people who have created it.

The stories of how great (and, sometimes, not-so-great) records came into being, and the trials and triumphs of singers and groups, are the basis of this book. You won't find much unconnected or useless trivia; I'm not really interested in who had the most gold records in 1993 or what label sold the most albums in 1967. But if you want to know about artists who have had their songs censored by the authorities, or argue about who the "Fifth Beatle" really was, or see a list of 10 rock songs lifted from classical music, this book is for you!

A few quick terms for those too young to remember the way music used to be transmitted—on records:

LPs were what today are called "CDs." Phonograph albums, or LPs, were full-length releases, usually about 20 minutes on each side. Today, because of the amount of space on a CD, artists are asked to put more music on each release than they used to.

45s were singles, with one song on each side of a seven-inch record with a big hole in the middle. **EPs**, mostly a phenomenon of Great Britain and other foreign lands, were seven-inch records containing four or five songs. They had a very *small* hole in the middle.

Here's a quick run-through of how a song gets onto a CD:

Songs are written and arranged by a band or a singer, then recorded in a **studio,** either onto thick, high-quality recording tape or directly onto a computer hard drive. Both forms of recording allow for **overdubbing**—that is, for several different **tracks** to be laid down in sequence and **mixed** to different levels on the finished recording.

The CD is then pressed up at a processing plant and given a cover design. Record companies, known also as **labels,** send out **promotional CDs** to **radio stations, publicists, disc jockeys,** and **publications** to get the media excited about the artist. Sometimes, illegal **payoffs** are made to get records played on the radio, videos spun on TV, and songs played in clubs. (Knowing this shouldn't dim your enjoyment of the music itself, but it's good to remember that, as in any industry, music has its own set of rule-breakers and shysters. You'll read about some of them here, but I'm *not* dedicating this book to crooks, hit men, or music-industry lawyers.)

On the other hand, the musicians whose stories fill these pages deserve my deep if hardly adequate thanks. I don't know who, what, or where I'd be without music. It's not a stretch to say that rock & roll saved me.

So here we are. It takes a lot of people to make a book, and so many people have given of their time and wisdom in the creation of this one that it's hard to count them all.

Several dear friends helped with ideas, suggested changes, or read early drafts of this material. Thanks, alphabetically, to Clark Besch, Mark Caro, Paul Fromberg, Phillip Hall, Ted Harris, Frank Kras, Bob Purse, Rob Rodriguez, Tom Shea, and Doug Tonks.

Don McKeon of Brassey's took a leap of faith in publishing this book, and he has my lasting thanks. He also knows a lot about rock music, which kept me on my toes!

My parents, brothers, and step-parents, my extended relatives, and my in-laws have shared music with me over the years, and they have my undying gratitude and love. Marco Antonio Garibay and Carolina Margaret Garibay are my special angels.

Other irreplaceable friends who have shared music with me include David and Stephanie Altman, Kathy Baum, Gail Edington, Larry Epke, Vicki and Gary Gillette, Leslie Goldberg, Jim Harp, Paul Hippensteel, all at Illuminous Ras, Joel Irono, Ken Kurson, Marty McCormack, Tim

McLoraine, Lisa Mikita, Jim Newberry, Ann-Marie Olson, Carroll Piper, Jim Piper, Tom Purcell, Shannon and Josh, Sheila Spica, Shannon Spica, Joan Spoerl, and the Fiendish Thingies: Lynn, Karen, Suz, Pam, Annette, and Sam.

Thanks also to Gary Gillette, Chris Karhl, and Greg Spira for their professional guidance and kindness, and to Jim Newberry for his terrific photographs.

Finally, I honor my brilliant and beautiful wife Cecilia Garibay, whose love, respect, support, and endless great ideas about music and musicians have helped make my life—to say nothing of this book—an amazing experience. I love you, Ceci.

And thank you, God.

Drowned

While "Don't drink the water" may be good advice for musicians on tour, "Don't even go *in* the water" might be even better advice. Too many rockers have lost it all on ill-advised trips into the deep—or even the shallows.

1. JOHNNY BURNETTE

Born in 1934, Burnette, his brother, Dorsey, and friend Paul Burlison made up the Rock 'n' Roll Trio, a powerhouse that cut some of the best rockabilly ever. Johnny, born in Memphis, had a short career as a boxer but was better suited to singing. His deep, expressive voice was at home on both rockers and ballads.

However, after some initial success, the trio's popularity faded in 1957, and the Burnette brothers began selling songs to other singers. Ricky Nelson turned several Burnette songs, including

"It's Late" and "Believe What You Say," into major hits.

That success led to a contract for Johnny, who scored four Top 20 hits in 1960–61, the most famous of which was the Sherman Brothers' "You're 16 (You're Beautiful, and You're Mine)." Burnette was even bigger in England.

When Burnette (oddly) began recording songs written by others, including future stars David Gates and P.J. Proby, the hits dropped off.

He took some time off to plan a comeback. Fishing on California's Clear Lake on August 14, 1964, Burnette sat on his tiny boat in the dusk. A bigger boat, a cruiser, raced through, and didn't see his unlit small craft. Thrown from the boat, Burnette drowned.

His music remains popular, especially in rockabilly-crazed Europe. Johnny's son, Rocky, even had a Top 10 song on the American charts in 1980, the '50s-inspired "Tired of Toein' the Line."

2. SHORTY LONG

Shorty Long, one of Motown's forgotten artists, was responsible for some of the funkiest music of the '60s. But if he is remembered today at all, it is for a comedy hit inspired by a TV show.

Born in 1940, the five-foot-tall Frederick Long (ergo the nickname) signed with Tri-Phi Records in 1962. Two years later, Long recorded his first single for Motown. His composition "Devil with a Blue Dress" later became a hit for a white soul band, Mitch Ryder and the Detroit Wheels. Long also released "Function at the Junction," which didn't sell much in 1966 but is now considered a classic.

In 1968, Long recorded "Here Comes the Judge," a novelty disc based on a line from TV's *Laugh-In* show uttered by comedian Dewey "Pigmeat" Markham. Despite a competing version from Markham, Long's recording of the song reached #8 on the charts in June 1968.

Long's star blazed brightly, but briefly. He recorded "Here Comes Fat Albert," based on Bill Cosby's comedy routine, but it wasn't a big success. On June 29, 1969, Long drowned when his boat capsized off Sandwich, Ontario, on the Detroit River.

Fortunately, a recent CD of Long's best work has spawned a revival.

3. BRIAN JONES

By 1969, Brian Jones of the Rolling Stones was thoroughly wasted. An endless procession of drugs, women, and alcohol contributed to his already borderline personality. He was abusive to his friends, lovers, and bandmates, and ill prepared to contribute either on stage or in the studio. Jones also mourned that the band, which he had started, had become Mick Jagger and Keith Richards's brainchild.

By this time all but barred from recording with the group, Jones left the Stones in June 1969. During that summer, Jones commissioned work on his estate house at Cotchford Farm, previously owned by *Winnie the Pooh* author A.A. Milne. A cadre of tough-guy homebuilders and workmen lived on the property, and many of them apparently harbored resentment of Jones's wealth and behavior.

On the night of July 3, Jones drowned in his pool; his body was found by his then-girlfriend, Anna Wohlin. Rumors quickly spread that some of Jones's employees were either responsible for his death or did nothing to prevent it. Money disappeared from Jones's accounts after his death, and some evidence relating to the case was destroyed.

Two recent books—*The Murder of Brian Jones* and *Who Killed Christopher Robin?*—have investigated the gory details, but it is unlikely that the case will be re-opened.

4. **RANDY CALIFORNIA**

Songwriter and guitarist for the late '60s–early '70s band Spirit, who had big hits with "I Got a Line on You," "Nature's Way," and the *Twelve*

Dreams of Dr. Sardonicus album, Randy California was born Randy Craig Wolfe. His mother married drummer Ed Cassidy (related to cowboy legend Hopalong Cassidy), and son and stepfather formed Spirit in 1967. California was just 16, while Cassidy, an explosive drummer with a jazz background, already had nearly 40 years under his belt.

California played with different lineups of Spirit for 30 years and made several solo albums. Unfortunately, on January 2, 1997, off Molokai, Hawaii, California and his 12-year-old son, Quinn, were overcome by waves while swimming. Although father pushed son to safety, he was swept away and never found.

Friends held a memorial service for California in Ventura, California, with music enthusiast Dr. Demento (a former Spirit roadie) reading the eulogy. It's fitting that Randy California, a man who loved nature and often sang about it, died in the sea.

5. JEFF BUCKLEY

Jeff Buckley's unusual guitar playing and singing brought him more fame in a four-year span than his late father, folk/jazz singer Tim Buckley, had throughout his 10-year career. After a live EP, *Live at Sin-E,* and a studio CD, *Grace,* Buckley the younger quickly acquired a reputation as a perfectionist who wouldn't let anything escape the studio unless it was pristine.

In May 1997, the 30-year-old Buckley was in Memphis, doing post-production work on music recorded with producer Tom Verlaine, formerly of the seminal '70s band, Television. After dinner on May 29, he and a friend were walking by Memphis's downtown harbor. Ever impulsive, Buckley decided—while fully clothed—to have a swim. He disappeared in the wake of some passing boats, and his body was found a week later.

It's not clear whether Buckley meant to commit suicide. He had sung about the subject in very painful terms in "Last Goodbye," but it is just as likely that Buckley died by misadventure.

The songs he was working on at the time were mixed posthumously by friend Chris Cornell, lead singer of the Seattle hard-rock band, Soundgarden. The album, released as *(Sketches) For My Sweetheart the Drunk* in 1998, did not dim Buckley's legacy.

6. DENNIS WILSON

Wilson, his brothers, Carl and Brian, and cousin Mike Love played in high school bands in the late '50s and early '60s. Settling on the Beach Boys name in 1962, they quickly learned to combine Four Freshmen-style harmonies with Chuck Berry riffs and topical lyrics about surfing and cars.

While Brian Wilson became the group's song-writing genius, Dennis Wilson (the band's only surfer) stood out for his All-American good looks, thumping drumming, and expressive voice. He was the band's true teen idol.

As the '60s progressed, Dennis Wilson began writing songs that showed a gentle but ominously insecure side. His efforts helped hold together later BB albums such as *Sunflower, Friends,* and *20/20.* Unfortunately he also discovered hard drugs and became involved with psychopath Charles Manson.

Wilson, like many '60s rockers, struggled to find his place in the '70s. He went through four wives, fathered four kids, and had a torrid affair with Fleetwood Mac's Christine McVie. He suffered bouts of depression and anger and temporarily lost his voice. On December 28, 1983, Wilson drunk-enly threw some personal items off his boat (docked at Marina del Rey) and drowned in shal-low water after diving to retrieve them. He was 39.

The tragic irony of the group's only surfer dying at sea could hardly be lost. When the Beach

Boys were renewed during the '90s, Wilson's raw but tender voice and underrated songwriting were missed.

7. JIM HODDER

Who sang lead on Steely Dan's first-ever single, in 1972? It wasn't regular lead singer/keyboardist Donald Fagen, or even the group's early second vocalist, David Palmer.

It was drummer Jim Hodder, whose strong tones graced the unsuccessful 45 "Dallas." He also sang the excellent "Midnight Cruiser" on the Dan's debut LP, *Can't Buy a Thrill.*

Hodder's solid Latin-influenced beat powered the first two Dan LPs before he was eased out during the recording of the group's third album, 1974's *Pretzel Logic.* In fact, the entire band was dissolved as Fagen and Walter Becker chose instead to rely on session musicians.

Hodder settled down in California and lived the ex-rock star life before drowning in his pool at his Point Arena, California, home on June 15, 1990. He was 42.

8. WILLIAM SINNOTT

Scottish bassist Wil Sin, born William Sinnott, joined the Shamen in 1988. The British band,

originally a psychedelic rock combo named Alone
Again Or (after a classic song by '60s band Love),
moved more toward the dance music underground
when Sinnott came aboard.

Sinnott's tech-savvy, electronic bent led the
Shamen to experiment with acid house beats.
The druggy ambience of the late '80s British rave
scene lent itself to the Shamen's music.

By 1991, the band was on the cusp of international success, touring with a multimedia show
that included slide projections, lights, films, DJs,
and taped samples. However, Sinnott wouldn't live
to see the band's explosion into stardom. On May
23, 1991, during a Canary Islands vacation, he
drowned off the island of Gomera.

The Shamen continued on, releasing "Move Any
Mountain" as a tribute to Sinnott. The song became
the band's first U.S. Top 40 hit. Other massive
dance hits followed, including "Boss Drum," "L.S.I.,"
and the not-so-subtle drug anthem, "Ebenezer
Goode."

9. KIRSTY MacCOLL

During the '80s and '90s, Kirsty was one of
Britain's most respected vocalists. She sang
material by such diverse talents as the McGarrigle
Sisters, the Smiths, and Billy Bragg; penned the

Tracey Ullman hit, "They Don't Know;" and hit the charts with her own "There's a Guy Works Down the Chipshop (Swears He's Elvis)."

She also guested on the Pogues' British hit, "Fairytale in New York," and the Smiths' last single, "Ask," and worked with the Rolling Stones.

The 41-year-old MacColl, daughter of folksinger Ewan MacColl and ex-wife of big-time record producer Steve Lillywhite, was swimming off the coast of Cozumel, Mexico, on December 18, 1999, when she was struck by a speedboat traveling in an area off-limits to boats. She died just feet away from her two sons.

MacColl had just completed an album of Cuban music as well as a TV documentary on Cuban musicians.

10. SCOTT SMITH

Vancouver-based Loverboy were mighty popular in the early '80s. The leather-clad pop-rockers scored nine U.S. Top 40 hits during the decade, with "Working for the Weekend" and "This Could be the Night" gracing many a high school prom.

The band took a break after the hits stopped, but returned in 1997. In November 2000, bassist Scott Smith, his girlfriend, Yvonne Mayotte, and a friend, Bill Ellis, began a sailing excursion from Vancouver to Los Angeles.

By November 30, the boat had gone as far south as San Francisco Bay. While Mayotte and Ellis were below in the ship's cabin, Smith was at the wheel, four miles offshore. Suddenly, a 25-foot wave knocked the 37-foot boat on its side. There was no sign of Smith, and the ship's wheel was torn off by the force of the blow.

While Smith was a skilled sailor and swimmer, the Pacific Ocean waters were cold and choppy, making it difficult for anyone to survive. His body was never found, even after Loverboy singer Mike Reno rented tugboats to trawl the area.

Sue Me, Sue You Blues

S hakespeare wrote, "First thing we do, let's kill all the lawyers." Plenty of musicians would agree—at least, the ones sued for plagiarism. The following cases have wildly differing outcomes, at least in part because the U.S. Supreme Court generally has refused to become involved in copyright cases.

1. THE CHIFFONS/GEORGE HARRISON

George Harrison's "My Sweet Lord," a single released from his first solo LP, *All Things Must Pass,* was a worldwide #1 in 1970.

Following the single's release, someone realized that some of the melody and chord changes of "My Sweet Lord" mirrored those of The Chiffons' 1963 smash "He's So Fine," written by Ronnie Mack.

Bright Tunes, publishers of "He's So Fine," sued Harrison for plagiarism, but the British singer claimed that any plagiarism was unconscious. The irony, of course, was thick; the Beatles have been ripped off, directly and indirectly, more than any other rock act.

Harrison's ex-bandmate, John Lennon, believed that Harrison "knew what he was doing" when he penned "He's So Fine," but also mocked the idea that anyone "owns" music. In 1973, Harrison wrote "Sue Me, Sue You Blues" about the legal miseries surrounding the final days of the Beatles (as well as the Bright lawsuit).

Three years later, as the Bright lawsuit ground to its finish, Harrison penned "This Song," in which he punned, "This tune/has nothing bright about it" and included a bass guitar break cheekily resembling those of the great soul records of the '60s. In the background, Monty Python-esque ladies' voices note that the bass notes are lifted from either "Rescue Me" or "I Can't Help Myself." The promotional film for "This Song," shot in a courtroom, portrayed close friend Harry Nilsson as a bailiff carting Harrison off to jail.

After a protracted trial, Harrison was found guilty of unconscious plagiarism on September 7, 1976, and ordered to pay $587,000 to Bright Tunes. To make matters worse, former Beatles

George Harrison holds a Beatles button while talking with fans in the 1970s.

manager Allen Klein bought Bright Tunes' publishing rights, and with it the right to continue to sue Harrison if he so desired.

2. GILBERT O'SULLIVAN/BIZ MARKIE

The culture of sampling—using someone else's previously recorded sounds on one's own record—can make for strange bedfellows. Perhaps none are weirder than singer/rapper Biz Markie and '70s vintage soft-rocker Gilbert O'Sullivan.

Markie, well known as a "human beat box," released an album in 1991 entitled, *I Need a Haircut.* One cut from the LP, "Alone Again," features the melody line and title phrase from cloth-capped British balladeer O'Sullivan's 1972 smasheroo "Alone Again (Naturally)." Permission was not sought from O'Sullivan's publishers to use the song, and no royalty arrangement was made. As a result, it wasn't too long before O'Sullivan's publishers sued.

Because of the lawsuit, Markie's album was recalled after its initial print run was sold and then pressed again without the offending track. Markie obviously was burned by the experience; his next CD was titled *All Samples Cleared!* Acts sampling songs from others usually go to great pains nowadays to obtain legal clearance and avoid such lawsuits.

3. JOHN LEE HOOKER/ZZ TOP

Who "writes" blues songs or folk songs? Does any one person deserve credit for songs that have undergone decades of appropriation and reinterpretation? These questions had a test case in the rock world of the '80s.

The late John Lee Hooker, one of the fathers of modern blues, penned "Boogie Chillun" in the late '40s, along with Bernard Besman. Hooker recorded the song in 1948 and 1950, then again in 1970 in collaboration with rockers Canned Heat.

Meanwhile, Texas rockers ZZ Top, well versed in the blues, had their first big hit with 1973's "La Grange." Some 17 years later, Besman (then well into his 80s), who owned the copyright to "Boogie Chillun," decided to sue ZZ Top for ripping off his song. "La Grange" had apparently only recently entered his sphere.

By the time the suit came to trial in 1996, a judge dismissed the claim made for the 1948 and 1950 recordings of "Boogie Chillun," noting that the two recordings were old enough to have fallen into the public domain. However, the 1970 Hooker/Canned Heat recording could still have been plagiarized—the jury could still be out.

While "Boogie Chillun" was clearly based on a timeworn formula of folk/blues construction, ZZ

Top's rewrite is based on the same formula. The two sides settled the suit for an undisclosed amount in 1997. Still unanswered is the question: Who writes blues songs?

4. RON SELLE/THE BEE GEES

The late '70s were, in general, good times to be a Bee Gee. A string of hit albums had made the vibrato-voiced Australian siblings the world's hottest act, and the punk rock backlash that would sink the act in the '80s was still to come.

However, storm clouds appeared on the horizon in the form of one Ron Selle, a suburban Chicago songwriter and choral music arranger. On March 29, 1980, Selle filed suit in Chicago against the Bee Gees, claiming that their 1977 multimillion-seller, "How Deep Is Your Love?" was stolen from his home-demo composition, "Let it End."

Selle, a lounge-type singer whose song bore fleeting melodic resemblance (and no stylistic resemblance) to the Bee Gees' hit, claimed that he had submitted his song for the group's perusal.

Unexplained was why Selle thought the Bee Gees, who rarely performed anyone else's songs, would bother to listen to an obscure demo by an outside songwriter. Selle's expert witness admitted under questioning that he had little familiarity with pop music or the Bee Gees.

Despite this, a jury—probably swayed by the case's David vs. Goliath scenario—ruled in favor of Selle in 1983. As the result was read, Robin Gibb shouted, "That verdict is a lie!" The judge agreed and overturned it. In his opinion, Selle had failed to prove the Bee Gees had seen or heard his material, making any plagiarism claim invalid.

5. CAROL HINTON/STEVIE NICKS

It galled Stevie Nicks of Fleetwood Mac to hear in 1980 that she was being sued for allegedly stealing the lyrics to "Sara," one of her most personal songs.

"Sara," the biggest hit from the multiplatinum *Tusk* album, was released in 1979. Two years later, a Ms. Carol Hinton of Rockford, Michigan, filed a claim against Nicks and Fleetwood Mac.

Hinton noted that she had sent Warner Brothers, the Mac's record company, lyrics to a song called "Sara" in fall 1978, before the album was released. Some of her lyrics were somewhat similar to Nicks's. However, in response, Nicks submitted a work tape of her song that was made in July 1978, making Ms. Hinton's argument somewhat irrelevant.

As in the Bee Gees/Ron Selle case, it is odd that anyone would think that Fleetwood Mac, a band that included three accomplished singer/songwriters, would have any interest in unsolicited material from outsiders.

"I don't deny that those were the words that she wrote," Nicks said years later. "But don't deny that those [the ones released] were the words that *I* wrote."

To end what could have been an ugly court battle, Nicks's lawyers settled by issuing Ms. Hinton a check for $1,500. Even now, Nicks fields questions from the press about the case.

6. HUEY LEWIS/RAY PARKER, JR.

Former country singer/hippie dropout Huey Lewis finally cashed in during 1984. He and his band, the News, sold millions of copies of their second album, *Sports,* which yielded several hit singles, including "I Want a New Drug."

Some months later, veteran session guitarist and soul singer Ray Parker, Jr., was hired to write and sing the theme song for the soundtrack of an upcoming movie, *Ghostbusters.* When Parker's song came out, eventually reaching #1 in August 1984, more than a few people noticed a distinct similarity between Lewis's hit and Parker's newly composed movie theme.

A legal basis for a filing of copyright infringement gained more steam when an incriminating letter sent to Parker was produced. Said letter advised Parker that the film's producers wanted a song similar to "I Want a New Drug" and even specified that the song's distinctive electric guitar rhythm pattern should be imitated.

Lewis filed suit in 1984, and the case dragged on for 11 years before both sides issued a joint press release saying that the issue had been "resolved amicably."

Fast forward to 2001. During an interview for a VH-1 *Behind the Music* special, Lewis commented on the lawsuit. He said that the worst part of the affair was not that Parker had ripped off the song, but that the music industry itself sees songs as interchangeable and that money can ruin the integrity of an artist.

Lewis noted in the interview that "they, basically, bought it," implying that Parker and his lawyers paid to settle the lawsuit. This fact hadn't been divulged to the press back in 1995. As a result, Parker has sued Lewis for damages, claiming that discussion of the terms of the settlement was prohibited. The suit is pending.

7. U2/CASEY KASEM/NEGATIVLAND

Bay Area recording ensemble Negativland showed their healthy disgust for the music industry on CDs such as *Helter Stupid/The Perfect Cut* and *Escape from Noise.*

In 1991, they went one step further. Slapping together a goofy spoken version of U2's "I Still Haven't Found What I'm Looking For" with samples of CB radio, outtakes of *American Top 40* DJ Casey Kasem cursing, and other audio delights, the band issued a single on their longtime label, SST, under the title, "U2." The sleeve featured a photo of a U-2 spy plane.

U2's record company, Island, was not amused. The label immediately filed suit, claiming that Negativland's single was misleading buyers into thinking it was the long-awaited new album by U2.

Kasem also jumped into the fray, threatening to sue because the outtakes featuring him, which were damaging to his reputation as a wholesome family entertainer, had never been licensed for release.

All existing copies of the CD were withdrawn and destroyed, as were the master recordings. However, some Negativland sympathizers in Canada have released unauthorized versions of the single on cassette and CD.

Fascinated by copyright law, Negativland made the case into a First Amendment cause célèbre. In doing so, they bankrupted themselves and lost the rights to several of their early recordings in a bitter fight with SST, which both dropped them from the label and sued them. Meanwhile, U2's lack of enthusiasm for prosecuting their fellow artists showed how much music industry lawyers were really running the show.

At one point, U2 guitarist The Edge found himself in a phone interview with *Mondo 2000* magazine concerning the band's use of pirated television images in their "Zoo TV" tour. In true commando style, one of the interviewers was Negativland's Mark Hosler. The Edge responded with good humor, agreeing that the use of TV images and song fragments weren't that different. Island eventually dropped its lawsuit.

However, the song was never reissued legitimately because Kasem wouldn't allow his outtakes to be used.

8. ROY ORBISON/2 LIVE CREW

Luther Campbell of 2 Live Crew parodied the lyrics of Roy Orbison and William Dees's "Oh, Pretty Woman" on the 1989 album, *As Clean as They Wanna Be*. He had been refused permission to use a sample of the song by Acuff-Rose,

Orbison's publisher, but then inserted the track on the CD anyway. He was immediately sued by Acuff-Rose for using the song without permission.

The case went all the way to the U.S. Supreme Court. At issue wasn't whether 2 Live Crew's version of "Oh, Pretty Woman" was dirty (it was), but rather whether artists have the right to parody published works and use existing art as the basis for other art.

Free-thinking music fans argued that other disciplines, such as painting and film, routinely use source material as the basis for collage, one of the great art forms of recent times.

In November 1993, the court ruled unanimously that 2 Live Crew's use of the song was protected by copyright law's "fair use" clause. This clause allows source material to be used in social commentary or parody as long as rights fees for sampling or use are paid.

Justice David Souter wrote that the Campbell version of the song could be intended "as a comment on the naiveté of the original . . . as a rejection of its sentiment that ignores the ugliness of street life and the debasement that it signifies."

9. CHUCK BERRY/JOHN LENNON

The Beatles' 1969 album, *Abbey Road,* led off with "Come Together," which opened with the lines, "Here come old flat-top/He come groovin' up slowly."

When music publisher Mo Levy, head of Roulette Records, heard the song, he immediately knew those words sounded familiar; they were from Chuck Berry's "You Can't Catch Me," written in 1956.

Of course, the line had nothing to do with the rest of the song, which sounded nothing like "You Can't Catch Me." But Levy, a tough guy with alleged Mafia connections, spent his career acquiring publishing rights to songs to control as much of the music industry as he could. He sued in early 1970.

Oddly, when Levy and John Lennon met, they liked each other. Levy respected the ex-Beatle's talent, while Lennon enjoyed Levy's New York street smarts. To appease Levy, Lennon agreed to record "You Can't Catch Me" (and two other songs Levy owned) for an oldies-but-goodies album to be produced by Phil Spector.

Then, everything got muddy. The *John Lennon: Rock & Roll* sessions dragged on while an apparently drunk Spector caused innumerable delays. Levy, growing impatient for the songs to be released (and to claim his royalty check), later claimed that Lennon gave him tapes to release on his own TV mail-order label, Adam VIII.

Worried that Levy might exact revenge for the delay, Lennon said he only wanted Levy to *hear* the tapes to gauge the progress of the recording sessions.

Shortly after Levy was lent the tapes, late-night TV ads appeared touting an Adam VIII album, *Roots.* The cover featured a blurred, poor-quality photo of Lennon, while the record itself consisted of terrible-sounding versions of the songs recorded by Spector. Levy had simply recorded the copy of the reel-to-reel Lennon lent him and pressed the songs onto poor-quality vinyl, stuffed the discs in a sleeve, and marketed them without permission.

Both Lennon and the folks on his label, Capitol, were incensed at this breach of faith and contract. They sued the unauthorized album right off the market. In April 1977, Lennon was awarded more than $80,000 in damages.

10. THE ISLEY BROTHERS/MICHAEL BOLTON

Michael Bolton's histrionic vocal style and frequent use of classic R&B songs gained him millions of fans—as well as the disdain of nearly as many who can't stand him.

The curly-tressed soul belter had availed himself of key nuggets of soul music in the past. When he was sued in 1992 for allegedly ripping off the Isley Brothers' "Love Is a Wonderful Thing" for his own song of the same name, the situation elicited more than a few guffaws.

In 1994, a California judge sent the case to a jury, which ruled that the Isley Brothers had been ripped off. The jury found that five essential parts of the song, including the fadeout and the title phrase were uncomfortably similar, both lyrically and musically. Bolton appealed, but the appellate court upheld the earlier ruling.

In January 2001, the Supreme Court (as it has in the past) refused to become involved in a copyright infringement case and let the appeals court ruling stand: Sony Music, Bolton, and co-author Andrew Goldmark were liable to the Isleys for $5.4 million. That figure includes two-thirds of the profits from Bolton's song and more than a quarter of the profits from the album that included "Love Is a Beautiful Thing."

This windfall proved to be a life raft for the Isleys, who, through mismanagement of their assets, had ended the year 2000 around $5 million in debt.

Didn't Want to Have to Do It

What makes a good record? What makes a hit? Sometimes the artists know, sometimes not.

1. "MIXED-UP CONFUSION," BOB DYLAN

This fascinating chunk of rockabilly was cut in November 1962, between Dylan's first and second albums. It was his first foray into rock & roll, released by Columbia in the wake of the heady buzz generated by his first album.

Unfortunately, the song wasn't successful by the artist's standards and was withdrawn from sale almost immediately. Years later, Dylan disowned the track, claiming to have written it in a taxicab on the way to the recording studio. "I'm not sure what I based this one on . . . I didn't arrange the session. It wasn't my idea."

2. *"HOW DO YOU DO IT?"* THE BEATLES

After their first single, "Love Me Do," was a moderate hit in Britain, producer George Martin searched for a sure-fire commercial song that would propel the Beatles to the top of the hit parade. Veteran songscribe Mitch Murray proferred "How Do You Do It?"

But the Beatles made their first of many risky career moves: they told Martin they hated the song.

Martin prevailed on the boys to record "How Do You Do It?" anyway, but the results were so unenthusiastic (the song remained unreleased until 1995) that Martin agreed to let them have a go at one of their own numbers.

Once that song, "Please Please Me," became a British #1 hit, Martin never questioned his group's judgment. And it is to the Beatles' credit that they took Martin's excellent suggestion to convert "Please Please Me" from a Roy Orbison-like dirge to a full-out rocker.

Another of Martin's groups, Beatle-friends Freddie and the Dreamers, had no problem accepting the gift of "How Do You Do It?"; they recorded it later in 1963 and racked up *their* first #1 hit.

3. "GREEN TAMBOURINE," THE LEMON PIPERS

Sometimes bands *don't* know best. The Lemon Pipers, from Oxford, Ohio, had released three flop singles on the Buddah label and, in late 1967, were about to be let go by the record company.

The label agreed to release another Lemon Pipers 45 on one condition: that the song be written and produced by Shelley Pinz and Paul Leka.

Leka, a pianist and composer, had already penned "Like Falling Sugar," an almost-hit in 1966 for the Palace Guard. He would later produce the Left Banke and play in Harry Chapin's band. Lyricist Shelley Pinz read a newspaper story about an elderly man in London who played music on the street and left a tambourine on the sidewalk to collect donations. Thus a "green tambourine."

The Lemon Pipers were horrified. They hated the song, preferring more progressive original material. However, they wanted to stay signed, so the group bit its collective tongue and agreed to work with Leka and Pinz.

"Green Tambourine," a highly commercial psychedelic-styled novelty featuring a catchy sitar riff, some goofy percussion, swirly, faux-Eastern strings, and a quasi-Arabic drum fadeout, became a #1 song in February 1968.

Nothing the Lemon Pipers released in its wake reached the Top 40, and the fivesome broke up the next year.

4. "DAYDREAM BELIEVER," THE MONKEES

When the Monkees recorded this John Stewart song in mid-1967 (Peter Tork dreaming up the introductory piano lick), singer Davy Jones had nothing but reservations about both the song and his performance.

First off, Jones hated the lyrics: "I kept asking Chip [Douglas, producer] what the words meant, and he said, 'Don't worry, just sing them.' I mean, 'Cheer up, sleepy Jean, what more can it mean to *a daydream believer and a homecoming queen*'?"

Jones also felt the instrumental backing was in a key that made it nearly impossible for him to sing. (He still winces, to this day, at some of his notes.) It took him several takes to get the song, and an irritated exchange between Jones and Douglas was left on the beginning of the record— which, lyrical and musical reservations from the singer aside, became the Monkees' third and final #1 hit in November 1967.

5. "MIND GARDENS," THE BYRDS

The Byrds, still one of the nation's top groups in early 1967, were constantly racked by dissension. At times, the group's creative tension resolved into unearthly collaborations replete with energy and beauty. At other times, the four lads just couldn't wait to punch each other out.

Some of their best songs are on their fourth album, *Younger than Yesterday,* but one track, David Crosby's "Mind Gardens," produced a squall of discontent.

The song, an allegory about how fear serves to close people off from the world, was almost too much. Free-flowing, formless, and festooned with a stream of guitar tracks recorded and played back backward, "Mind Gardens" was sung by Crosby in a histrionic voice that veered into hippie self-parody.

The rest of the band resented having to play on the song. Lead guitarist Roger McGuinn, vocal in his disgust for "Mind Gardens," later remarked, "Even Crosby copped that it was a bummer." Not true; Crosby defends the song to this day.

6. "IT WOULD BE SO NICE," PINK FLOYD

In early 1968, Pink Floyd needed a hit single. The departure some months before of Syd Barrett, the fledgling band's lead guitarist, singer, and chief songwriter, had left the Floyd hard-pressed for commercial material.

Keyboardist Rick Wright brought in a pleasant, inconsequential chunk of psychedelic fluff entitled, "It Would Be So Nice." Short of songs, the other three members of the band gulped hard and recorded it, with Wright singing lead. The performance was okay, if somewhat unenthusiastic, but the single died quickly on the charts.

"I don't like the song or the way it's sung," bassist Roger Waters said later. "Bloody awful, wasn't it?" summed up drummer Nick Mason. This was just one opening salvo in a fight that eventually would estrange Wright from the rest of his bandmates by the mid-'70s.

7. "NA NA HEY HEY, KISS HIM GOODBYE," THE STEAM

Songwriters Gary DeCarlo and Dale Frasheur were busy writing and recording singles for the Mercury label in 1969. Mercury wanted to release four singles by the duo, but needed some b-sides to fill out the records.

So, lifting some lyrics from the 1960 Jerry Butler hit, "He Will Break Your Heart," and welding them to a silly chant and a simple, xylophone-led musical backing, the two (along with songwriter friend Paul Leka) cut a quickie b-side in just a few minutes. All three thought that "Na Na Hey Hey, Kiss Him Goodbye," based on a song DeCarlo and Frasheur had performed long ago in another band, was a hunk of trash.

But when executives at Mercury heard the song, they thought it was a potential hit. Shocked and horrified, DeCarlo and Frasheur refused even to put their names on the record as artists, although they did claim a songwriting credit. Leka came up with the name, "Steam," as the new "group's" handle.

Disc jockeys soon began playing the oddly titled track, which went all the way to #1 in December 1969. Meanwhile, the songs DeCarlo and Frasheur had worked on so hard, and really wanted to release, were lost in the shuffle and never went anywhere on the charts.

When "Na Na Hey Hey, Kiss Him Goodbye" became a hit, DeCarlo and Frasheur refused to tour to promote it, leaving Leka to recruit several Connecticut musicians to become Steam.

8. "YOU AIN'T SEEN NOTHIN' YET," BACHMAN-TURNER OVERDRIVE

Coming off several hit singles and albums, BTO were a well-established group with good commercial judgment. But their biggest-ever song was a happy accident that almost never reached the ears of the public.

"You Ain't Seen Nothin' Yet" was written and recorded in early 1974 as a joke for guitarist and singer Randy Bachman's brother, Gary, who stuttered. An embarrassed Bachman didn't even think the song worthy of recording or release until the group's manager talked them into putting it on their upcoming album, then releasing it as a single.

Talk about surprise acts of genius. The song's Dave Mason-like jangly guitars, hard-rocking chorus, catchy title, and carefree lyrics were just right for the times, and "You Ain't Seen Nothin' Yet" became BTO's only #1 hit.

9. "(DON'T YOU) FORGET ABOUT ME," SIMPLE MINDS

British band Simple Minds were more than a bit uncomfortable with the idea of performing a song for the soundtrack of John Hughes's film *The Breakfast Club*. While they wanted the gig, they were songwriters themselves and didn't relish working with outside writers.

To make things more awkward for Simple Minds, Keith Forsey and Steve Schiff had originally penned "(Don't You) Forget about Me" with former Roxy Music singer Bryan Ferry in mind.

Simple Minds had enjoyed success in Britain, but had not crossed over to the American charts. This song was their big opportunity for exposure, and the band put down a good, if slick, recording despite its communal trepidation. Spurred up the hit parade by exposure in the film, "(Don't You) Forget about Me" eventually became a #1 hit in America in March 1985.

Singer Jim Kerr detested the lyrics, however, especially the line, "I'll be alone, dancin', you know it, baby." Kerr said that his lack of clear enunciation of that line and others in the song was because he hated the idea of singing words like "vanity," "insecurity," and "baby," and that he never would have written such words himself.

10. "I THINK WE'RE ALONE NOW," TIFFANY

Singer Tiffany Darwisch wasn't familiar with the 1967 Tommy James hit, "I Think We're Alone Now," when her manager, George Tobin, suggested she perform it in 1986. Initially, the 16-year-old didn't care for the song.

"I didn't hate it, but I wasn't crazy about it either," she told *Billboard* magazine. But the overt commerciality of Richie Cordell's classic paean to teenage lust and a slick, pumping arrangement soon convinced the not-yet-legal-age singer otherwise.

Promoted through Tiffany's innovative shopping-mall tour schedule and its resulting publicity, "I Think We're Alone Now" eventually broke through to radio and MTV and became her first #1 hit in November 1987.

Foreign Tongues

English is one of the most difficult tongues in the world to learn. However, because of its status as the world's premier cultural (and industrial) language, groups that want international acceptance almost always gear their product toward the English-speaking market.

1. LOS BRAVOS

A five-piece band consisting of four Spaniards and one German, Los Bravos racked up one large American (and English) hit, the British Invasion- and Motown-influenced "Black Is Black," in 1966.

Los Bravos' first English-language attempt after several Spanish-language hits, "Black Is Black" featured a vocal performance that nobody would have figured came from overseas.

The group's singer, German native Mike Kogel, later left and was replaced by Alan Anderson, brother of longtime Yes lead vocalist Jon Anderson (!). Los Bravos' story ends sadly with organist Manuel Fernandez's suicide, but the band did leave behind one classic.

2. CAN

A five-piece experimental act, influenced by James Brown, the Beatles, Frank Zappa, and various modern classical composers, Can coalesced in Cologne, Germany, in 1968.

Originally, American painter Malcolm Mooney (the only non-German in the band) was the lead singer, but after he left because of mental problems, Japanese exile Damo Suzuki, living on the streets of Munich, was asked to join. Homeless, possibly insane, and with nothing else to occupy his time, he agreed.

Suzuki, who had no training but possessed an undeniable, if odd, natural talent, sang on the four albums (1970–73) regarded as the group's best work: *Soundtracks, Tago Mago, Ege Bamyasi,* and *Future Days.* The underground aggregation even enjoyed a hit single in Germany, "Spoon," the theme of a popular TV show.

The group's liquid, pulsing instrumental work, and Suzuki's odd stream-of-consciousness lyrics, combining Japanese, English, and French, as well as frequent nonsense sounds, continue to influence.

3. SHOCKING BLUE

Guitarist Robbie van Leeuwen was a veteran of Holland's rock scene. When his band, Shocking Blue, added big-lunged brunette singer Mariska Veres in 1969, big-time success followed.

A catchy van Leeuwen song, "Venus," became a major European hit in 1969, and busted its way to the top of the American charts in February 1970. Despite Mariska's shaky pronunciation on "Venus," she did sound a little like Grace Slick, and the band's performance was confident.

The group followed up with "Mighty Joe," another fine rocker with some questionable English usage. It was the Shocking Blue's last American hit, although the band racked up European smashes until 1974.

4. KRAFTWERK

Not only did Kraftwerk have to learn how to sing in English, they had to learn how to become machines. Or was it learn how to become humans?

Two German musicians, Ralf Hutter and Florian Schneider, teamed up in 1970 to play music influenced by the factories that surrounded their community in Düsseldorf. With an innovative use of synthesizers, Kraftwerk (German for "powerplant") made liquid, arresting music that reflected the feel of industrialized modern Germany.

Hutter and Schneider claimed to be robots and, in their interviews, laid the credit for their music entirely on the machines they used to make it. By 1974, they had added two members to augment live performances.

By 1980's almost-hit single, "Pocket Calculator," Kraftwerk's use of heavily accented English had improved. (Their first American hit single, 1974's "Autobahn," was sung mostly in German.)

One of the groups responsible for techno (their 1977 album, *Trans-Europe Express,* is a major touchstone of dance music), Kraftwerk were undeniably one of the more forward-thinking bands of the '70s.

5. **ABBA**

In the '60s, Bjorn Alvaeus and Benny Anderson were well-known pop stars in their native Sweden, fronting the Hootenanny Singers and the Hepcats, respectively. At the same time, singers Anni-Frid Lyngstad and Agnetha Faltskog were successfully navigating the pop jungle.

By the early '70s, Benny and Anni-Frid had met and moved in together; Bjorn and Agnetha married the next year. A year or so later, the four friends undertook a joint musical project designed to maximize their talents.

Bjorn and Benny believed that their songs were worthy of international acceptance, so they chose to write lyrics in English. The ladies didn't know the language, so they had to learn to sing phonetically, with Bjorn and Benny breaking the words into Swedish syllables.

The result was more than palatable to the public. "Waterloo" won the 1974 Eurovision Song Contest and became the band's first international smash. From 1974 to 1982, ABBA (the first letters of each of their names) racked up dozens of worldwide hits, including 14 U.S. Top 40 records. The ladies sang lead on all of them except for 1979's uncharacteristically rocking "Does Your Mother Know?"

6. BLUE SWEDE

Led by veteran Swedish pop star Bjorn Skiffs, the punningly named seven-piece band, Blue Swede, made their mark on the American charts in 1974.

Their version of B.J. Thomas's 1969 hit, "Hooked on a Feeling," based on a 1972 recording by British popster Jonathan King, was certainly ear-catching. With its clunky, horn-led arrangement, sloppy reggae beat, and arresting "ooga-chaga" introduction, it was almost unidentifiable as having been anyone else's song, and sounded like nothing else on the radio at the time.

That Blue Swede's version of "Hooked on a Feeling" went all the way to #1, despite Skiffs's very poor English (probably learned in bits and pieces), was a tribute to the disc's off-the-wall commerciality.

The original lyric, "Got a bug from your girl, but I don't need no cure/I just stay addicted and hope I can endure," became, in Skiffs's hands, "Got a blot from you girl, but I don't need my cure/I just stay here fictin' if I can for sure."

The dangers of phonetic translation . . .

7. SHONEN KNIFE

Three young Japanese women—guitarist Naoko Yamano, her sister, Atsuko, on drums, and bassist Michie Nakatani—bonded in the '80s through their love for the Beatles, XTC, science fiction, animals, and '60s fashion as well as their interest in newer, punkier bands like the Ramones, Sonic Youth, and Redd Kross.

So, in true punk style, and in a most un-Japanese way, the ladies formed a band, Shonen Knife (roughly, "Boy Knife") and released low-budget recordings of simple but appealing songs. The lyrics' depth often outstripped Naoko and

Michie's ability to sing them, but part of the band's appeal was its amateurishness.

Singing in halting English about spaghetti with mushrooms, table-tennis-playing boyfriends, ecological disasters, and people turning into vegetables, Shonen Knife found their heroes loved their music as well. The band generated an underground buzz and eventually got an American record deal. Thurston Moore of Sonic Youth played guitar on their 1993 LP, *Rock Animals*.

The band went on several successful U.S. tours, appearing in matching '60s-styled outfits designed by Atsuko, making goofy sci-fi videos, and landing interviews in magazines like *Mondo 2000*.

8. STEREOLAB

Out of the ashes of forgotten band McCarthy came Stereolab, a (usually) six-piece unit revolving around the French/British husband/wife duo of singer and lyricist Laetitia Sadier and guitarist Tim Gane.

Musicwriter Gane and the band, which also included Australian backup singer Mary Hansen and future High Llama Sean O'Hagan, crafted songscapes from '60s French pop, experimental rock, and (later) Latin music and jazz, while Sadier's half-English, half-French lyrics were by turns intensely personal, coolly ironic, and politically savvy. Some of her songs with English-language titles were sung in French, and often, when she sang in English, her lyrics were nearly indecipherable.

Sadier has only printed lyrics to a few of Stereolab's songs, choosing to retain some mystery in her work. She is not afraid to write political lyrics, but rejects the interpretation that her work is purely Marxist.

9. SUPER FURRY ANIMALS

Gruff Rhys and Daf Ieuan of Cardiff, Wales, played in several local bands before hooking up with fellow Welsh band veterans Cian Ciaran, Guto Pryce, and Huw Bunford in 1993.

After two releases on Welsh independent Ankst (the first being the singularly titled EP, *Llanfairpwllgwyngyllgogerychwyndrobwllantys iliogogogochynygofod*), the Animals signed with Alan McGee's influential Creation label and put out four CDs, mixing songs in English with those in their native Welsh.

"We had to get over the taboo—and it was a taboo at the time [to sing in English]," Ieuan told *Mojo* magazine in 2001. "It was so politicized with the Welsh language, and it's taken people time to come around to it."

When Creation folded in 1999, the band chose to record an album *(Mwng)* entirely in Welsh, which, amazingly, nearly reached the Top 10 in Britain. The SFA reemerged in 2001 with the ambitious concept album, *Rings around the World.* International success still eludes the band, but it may be just a matter of time.

10. GORKY'S ZYGOTIC MYNCI

Hailing from Wales, Gorky's Zygotic Mynci (Welsh for "Dumb Reproductive Monkey") began as a bedroom band.

Siblings Euros (guitar) and Megan (violin) Childs, guitarist John Lawrence, bass player Richard James, and drummer Euros Rowlands were well-to-do kids who signed in the early '90s with Welsh label Ankst. There, they released three albums popular with the indie-rock crowd *(Patio, Tatay,* and *Bwyd Time)* before hooking up with Mercury Records in 1996.

Their indie-label singles were all in Welsh, but since they signed with Mercury, Gorky's have recorded most of their songs in English. They have since released five albums of pretty melodies and kitchen-sink arrangements, but have not yet broken the barrier in the United States.

The Fifth Beatle

While nobody but the Fab Four were responsible for their songwriting, vocal harmonies, and winning personalities, plenty of friends helped along the way and can be considered for honorary "Fifth Beatle" status. It's worth breaking our book's ten-item format to include this list—it's impossible to leave any of them off!

1. STUART SUTCLIFFE

A Liverpool art school pal of John Lennon's from Liverpool, Sutcliffe was the band's bass guitarist in the early days. He couldn't play the instrument and was never sure whether he even *belonged* in rock & roll, but he looked good, and John Lennon wanted him in.

When the band toured Germany, Sutcliffe met Astrid Kirchherr, who would become the love of his life. Preferring to concentrate on painting (and on Astrid), Sutcliffe left the band and stayed in Germany when the other four Beatles returned to Liverpool in mid-1961. Stu and Astrid were married that June in Hamburg.

Unfortunately, Sutcliffe died tragically of a brain hemorrhage in April 1962. He was only 21, and the world lost a potentially excellent painter.

2. PETE BEST

The Beatles' first full-time drummer, Pete Best, joined in August 1960. He was considered a good enough skin-pounder and the most conventionally handsome of the band.

Best's mother, Mona, owned the Casbah, a coffee club where the group occasionally played gigs. Given his fan support, looks, and connections, Best certainly felt that his status in the band was solid. However, when the Beatles came under Brian Epstein's guidance, Best began to fall from favor.

Tales of interband jealousy over Pete's legion of female fans may have some truth, but it appears that more germane reasons for his departure were his inability to handle more rhythmically tough material and his lack of enthusiasm for the Beatles' more European-style clothes, hair, and humor.

When EMI producer George Martin voiced objections about Best's stiff drumming, the other three Beatles took the opportunity to fire Best and bring in their friend, Ringo Starr. Or, rather, they asked Epstein, their *manager,* to fire Best.

3. KLAUS VOORMANN

A Beatle friend and musical accomplice dating back to the group's early days in Hamburg, Voormann may be best known in Fab Four circles for his classic cover illustration on the 1966 *Revolver* LP.

But he also had a memorable stint as bass player in Lennon's first solo project, the Plastic Ono band. Voormann played in the five-piece group that appeared at the 1969 Toronto Peace Concert, marking the first on-stage solo appearance by any Beatle. Later on, he also provided the rolling bass line on John's 1970 hit, "Instant Karma."

Voormann also produced some Beatles promotional videos, painted the cover for George Harrison's *Wonderwall Music* LP, and went on to play sessions for Lennon, Harrison, and Ringo Starr as well as other rockers of the '60s and '70s.

4. ASTRID KIRCHHERR

A woman as "Fifth Beatle"? Yes! Astrid is the person most responsible for one of the Beatles' most important innovations: their hair.

Astrid became a friend of the band and helped take care of them during their days in Hamburg. One day when the guys were all out swimming, Astrid noticed that their long, pompadour-style hair looked good when it hung, wet, over their foreheads.

From there, it wasn't long before a singular, European-influenced hairstyle was born—a style also influenced by the burgeoning gay pop culture of the early '60s of which the Beatles often found themselves on the periphery.

Astrid Kirchherr also turned out to be an outstanding photographer and has devoted much of her time in recent years to showing her photographs of the Beatles from the early '60s.

5. BRIAN EPSTEIN

Brian Epstein, a well-spoken, elegant gentleman who managed a Liverpool record store, prided himself on stocking any record that a customer wanted. In October 1961, he was unable to locate a record made in Germany by the Beatles, so he decided to find out more about the group.

Stumbling into a lunchtime performance at the dank, smelly Cavern Club on November 9, Epstein was hypnotized by the Beatles' stage presence. He quickly signed on to become their manager, despite no experience in administering to a rock group.

Throwing himself fully into his new venture, "Eppie" got the Beatles out of leather and into suits and began furiously hawking around their demo tapes. His tireless promotion for "his boys" led to a contract with Parlophone and, eventually, world domination.

It came at a price, however. Epstein, always insecure, had to hide his gay lifestyle from the public (although the Beatles themselves had no problem with it). He fell into drink and drugs and a series of unsuccessful affairs, and when the Beatles stopped touring in 1966, Epstein found himself less needed.

On August 27, 1967, Epstein was found dead at his home in London. He had accidentally overdosed on sleeping pills. He was just 32.

6. NEIL ASPINALL

To this day, Neil Aspinall remains part of the Beatles' inner circle.

An accountant by trade, Aspinall—originally a friend of Pete Best's—quit his job in 1961 at age

20 to work as the Beatles' road manager. In this position, he drove the band's van, hauled equipment, and fetched drinks.

As the group's popularity exploded, Aspinall found himself accompanying the Fabs around the world, receiving sports cars as Christmas gifts, helping to form Apple Records, and being drawn to the various subcultures in which the Beatles immersed themselves.

Aspinall remained close to the foursome after their breakup. He was largely responsible for the coordination of songs that made up the 1995 *Anthology* CD series and also had much of the responsibility for producing the best-selling *Anthology* hardcover book.

7. **MAL EVANS**

The beefy Evans, a onetime postal worker, was one of the band's trusted entourage as early as 1963 and stayed on the scene until they broke up.

Evans became a Beatles fan watching them at the Cavern, then joined Neil Aspinall on the road crew. He schlepped equipment on the Beatles' world tours, did personal errands for the foursome, appeared in the movies, *Help!* and *Let It Be,* and even took up the occasional instrument. (Completists may want to note that Evans banged the anvil on "Maxwell's Silver Hammer" and played one-note organ on the last verse of "You Won't See Me.")

After the Beatles splintered, Evans remained on the edges of rock music, but without the Fab Four, he seemed to lose his way. He experienced some drug problems and was mistakenly killed by overeager Los Angeles cops during a raid in 1974.

8. GEORGE MARTIN

A 35-year-old London-based staff producer for Parlophone Records, Martin found himself in June 1962 auditioning a pop foursome from Liverpool.

Unimpressed with the group's ramblings through blues standards and rock & roll chestnuts, Martin nonetheless was intrigued by the foursome's presence and energy. In September of that year, the Beatles recorded "Love Me Do," their first single.

With their next record, the #1 "Please Please Me," the Beatles' run of success had begun. Martin, who would produce all their albums, save *Let It Be,* was a major part of the band's success. He knew how to arrange strings and horns, was willing to try new ways of recording, and, just as important, had the Beatles' respect: he treated them as creative individuals and they respected his knowledge. Martin's background in recording comedy records with The Goons (Spike Milligan,

Peter Sellers, and Harry Secombe) also piqued the Fab's interest.

Martin was rightfully lauded for the technical brilliance behind such LPs as *Revolver* and *Sgt. Pepper's Lonely Hearts Club Band* and is still viewed as one of rock music's greatest producers.

9. MURRAY THE K

The only one on this list with the temerity to actually *call* himself "The Fifth Beatle," Murray "The K" Kaufman was a staggeringly popular New York disc jockey in the '50s and '60s.

As the first New York record-spinner to jump on the Beatles bandwagon, Murray the K used his connections with promoters and record companies to get special access to the Fab Four.

He offered the nascent hitmakers tons of publicity and airtime; the Beatles, in turn, enjoyed his company, humored him gracefully, and gave him plenty of material for his on-air hijinks. Kaufman quickly became the man for British bands to see in New York.

10. JIMMY NICOL

After Ringo Starr joined the group in 1961, Jimmy Nicol was the only other person ever to appear on a stage with the Beatles.

Nicol, an obscure British drummer, was tabbed to replace Ringo Starr on two short tours (to Scandinavia and the south Pacific) in June 1964. Starr was taken ill with tonsillitis on July 3 with the tour about to begin. If such a calamity happened today, a superstar group would simply cancel their appearances, but back then, everyone felt that The Show Must Go On.

So, with very little training, Nicol took over and, by all accounts, did a decent enough job during Beatles concerts in Copenhagen, Amsterdam, Hong Kong, and Adelaide. He then returned to total obscurity.

11. BILLY PRESTON

Occasionally, session musicians were credited when they played on Beatles records, but only Billy Preston was given equal billing.

The Beatles met Preston in the early '60s, when the American keyboardist was touring with one of their heroes, Little Richard. In early 1969, George Harrison (Preston's benefactor of sorts) thought that having a fifth musician would shore up the Fab Four's current back-to-the-basics project.

So Preston, visiting England at the time, came to the group's sessions. He played an electric piano solo on "Get Back," which was issued on a single in February 1969 and credited to "The Beatles with Billy Preston."

He also appeared in *Let It Be,* then signed a contract as a solo artist with the group's Apple label. Preston enjoyed several major hits, including "Will It Go 'round in Circles," "Outa Space," and "Nothing from Nothing" during the '70s. Later, he appeared at several Beatles fan conventions and recorded sporadically, but fell afoul of the law on several occasions.

I Want It All

From M&M's® and chewable vitamins to gardenia-scented hallways, more and more singers and groups are making strange and, sometimes, completely outrageous demands for backstage accommodations at shows (and even at photo opportunities). This isn't a new phenomenon, but it shows how crazy a business popular music has become that these requests are greeted with little more than a "ho-hum," then quickly fulfilled.

1. AEROSMITH

From their '70s days of drug and groupie excess to their current days of . . . well . . . groupie excess, Aerosmith members have willingly served as poster boys for sex, drugs, and rock & roll.

Tales of band members taking postconcert showers with nubile female fans, while wives waited merely feet away, are legendary. At one point, the group was reportedly demanding a huge vat of pasta following their gigs—presumably not for eating, but to frolic around in with the young ladies.

Finally, lead singer Steven Tyler (who is proud of his computer database of the women he's bedded on the road) can be just as much of a diva as any modern R&B queen, rebelling when anyone refers to him backstage as "Steve." Usually, guys named Steven are *happy* to have their names shortened.

2. VAN HALEN

Everyone in the rock music biz has heard of Van Halen's "M&M's®" rider. During the late '70s and early '80s, their contracts specified that their dressing room munchies spread had to include a bowl of M&M's® with the brown ones removed.

The band's defense of this clause is sensible: if promoters violated *that* minor item in the contract, then they hadn't read it carefully, and as a result might have violated *other* clauses.

And this indeed happened. In 1981, VH canceled a gig in Colorado because a promoter had not only left the brown M&M's® in, but also hadn't properly fortified the stage to carry the huge setup the band was trucking around. The decorations actually sank through the stage.

Nevertheless, David Lee Roth's description of his tantrum indicates that VH's lead singer fully enjoyed playing the spoiled child. "I found some brown M&M's®, I went into full Shakespearean '*What* is this before me?'... you know, with the skull in one hand... and promptly trashed the dressing room. Dumped the buffet, kicked a hole in the door, twelve thousand dollars' worth of fun."

Sometimes, all a child needs is an excuse.

3. **DIANA ROSS**

Just call her Miss Ross... if you have to speak to her at all.

Motown's Queen is a virtual tantrum machine who once bitched out her roadies in front of 50,000 fans at London's Wembley Stadium. A lady with few friends in the business, who was booed at former Supreme Florence Ballard's funeral, Diana has insisted in concert contracts that nobody standing backstage be allowed to make eye contact with her.

A summer 2001 appearance at the U.S. Open tennis tourney confirmed Ms. Ross's divahood. Lip-synching to a tape of "God Bless America," she forgot the words, turning her head to mask her embarrassment. She later sat in a private box to watch one of the tennis matches, but her hairdo was so large adjacent spectators had to shift in their seats.

4. JACKYL

A long-haired, raucous, raunchy, rockin' five-piece band from Georgia, Jackyl's newest slogan is, "Back again, bigger than life, and twice as ugly." Their latest LP, *Cut the Crap,* is representative of the band's screw-it-all attitude.

On tour, however, things seem to get a little odd, even for good ol' rockin' country boys. At one point in their career, the group's tour rider demanded a three-foot wooden barstool that the group was free to destroy as well as—yes, this is correct—a shaved gerbil.

It almost makes Jackyl's onstage mechanical bull and audience body-part autographing seem tame.

5. CHRISTINA AGUILERA

The teen queen requests (and gets) police escorts . . . and at age 16, she's an international star. A tour rider acquired by thesmokinggun.com revealed that perhaps Ms. Aguilera is still learning who she is—and what a girl really wants.

In addition to asking for a huge spread of organic food, herbal teas, and a platter full of chewing gum and breath mints, Ms. Aguilera requests plenty of items that would probably send her dietitians into shock.

Some of the haul includes all the Flintstones chewable vitamins she can suck down, bags of Oreos® and chocolate chip cookies, a container of nondairy coffee creamer, sandwiches on white bread, and a six-pack of cola.

6. **POSH SPICE (VICTORIA ADAMS)**

"Posh" indeed. After she and British footballer David Beckham took up residence together, British TV channel Grenada made plans to film a documentary about the celebrity couple.

However, Posh and Beckham made outrageous demands, even by the standards of their professions. The two wanted complete control over the content of the documentary (including rights to censor anything they didn't like), free will to hire and fire people working on the program, 40 percent of royalties from the show, and a one-time £50,000 payment.

A senior Grenada producer told the *Telegraph* newspaper, "It's incredible what celebrities like these two think they can get away with. Whether it is their management companies or the couple themselves behind this, they're behaving like little tin gods."

Grenada canceled the proposed documentary.

7. **REBA McENTIRE**

The queen of the adult-contemporary country set (and, now, TV comedienne hopeful) doesn't look or sing like a diva in the classic sense, but she is earning her stripes quickly—albeit in a dignified, nonviolent way.

A contract rider for one of La McEntire's recent tours specified that the plastic cups to be left in her dressing room had to be "absolutely clear, not opaque."

8. **JENNIFER LOPEZ**

It's hard to tell how rumors of divahood get started, but it's clear that in her brief career, J. Lo has acquired quite a reputation.

Even though she made fun of herself and her diva status on a February 2001 episode of *Saturday Night Live,* Lopez is deadly serious about her perks. She allegedly has submitted contract riders that include expensive perfumes to be sprayed in her path, a separate person to do nothing but blow-dry her hair, and a retinue of more than 50 friends and associates. No wonder concert tickets cost so much these days.

As in the case of Diana Ross, J. Lo has instructed her guards to ensure than nobody backstage or on location speaks with her or makes eye contact unless given prior clearance. Wouldn't want to have to connect with all the little people who help set up a stage show or a recording studio.

When Lopez was asked to appear on a version of Marvin Gaye's "What's Going On?" to benefit victims of the September 11, 2001, terrorist attacks in New York, she demanded a 45-foot-long trailer with enough food to feed her entire entourage. The trailer also had to come with a CD player (with several specified CDs), a VCR, a hair sink, and a makeup mirror.

More money had to be sucked away from the proceeds to provide Lopez with several varieties of fresh flowers and an elaborate furniture setup.

9. **MARIAH CAREY**

The popular soprano will only allow posed photos to be taken of one side of her face. She also brings along a towel-hander to her shows—yes, that's right, someone to do nothing but hand her dry towels—and keeps a steady supply of Cap'n Crunch cereal on hand at all times. Watch out for those teeth!

Mariah's summer 2001 nervous breakdown was just one sign of trouble. La Carey also appears to be a little jealous, insisting that posters of other female singers (Christina Aguilera et al.) be taken down wherever she appears.

In September 2001, she became angry at Jennifer Lopez, who sampled a piece of music that Carey had already sampled for one of *her* songs. A journalist from *Allure* magazine recently reported that when she said she'd talked to Lopez, Carey said, "I bet that was really intellectually stimulating. I bet you could just see the depth in her eyes."

Rowrr!

10. MADONNA

The Material One's backstage persona, cleaned up somewhat for her self-important, cloying "tell-all" film, *Truth or Dare,* may have understated her divahood just a touch. Or a ton.

Madonna stayed in New York for a spell in 2000. During that time, she actually had assistants repaint the walls of her hotel room in a softer shade to make it friendlier to the delicate one's vibrations.

Shortly afterward, she vacationed in Italy and asked that all the villa's floodlights be turned off in the evening so that she could better see the stars—at least those stars not named "Madonna."

It has also been reported that Luciano Pavarotti would like to sing a duet with her. Would there be enough room on one stage for the egos of both artists?

I'll Be Your Baby Tonight

Ever since Robert Zimmerman became Bob Dylan, then **BOB DYLAN**, in the mid-'60s, the industry has been searching for the next one. And the next one. And the one after that. Often against the will of the poor artist stuck with the tag, "the new Bob Dylan."

1. PHIL OCHS

Fellow New York folkie Phil Ochs didn't follow Dylan's mid-'60s path of love songs, rock instrumentation, and mainstream success. In fact, he criticized Dylan's movement from political folk into rock, which led to a rift between them.

Ochs, the author of classic protests such as "Too Many Martyrs," "I Ain't Marchin' Anymore," and "The Marines Have Landed on the Shores of Santo Domingo," made his mark with several LPs of topical political songs played on acoustic guitar.

A journalist by trade, Ochs wrote intensely urgent lyrics using metaphors and raw symbolism.

His beautiful personal songs, "Changes" and "When I'm Gone," were especially poignant because they were unexpected.

When he did abandon the solitary acoustic guitar, he went to full-blown baroque-style orchestral accompaniment on 1967's *Pleasures of the Harbor* LP. His commercial appeal waned as his songs became more insular. Ochs suffered bouts of depression and drank too much, and an odd 1970 revival as an Elvis Presley-style rocker didn't slow his decline.

Ochs's last major public appearance, coming two years before his 1976 suicide, was at a benefit concert to oppose the military government in Chile. He and Dylan shared the stage.

2. DONOVAN

A British folk/blues singer with an appealing, raspy voice and excellent finger-picking skills, Donovan Leitch leapt onto the scene in 1965. Hailed by the British press as a homegrown Dylan, he was, as a result, referred to as "Dylavan" by some cynical observers.

However, Donovan began to develop his own romantic-poet-influenced style with such sublime compositions as "Catch the Wind," "Colours," and "Summers Day Reflection Song."

Always much more personal than political, Donovan moved seamlessly into electric music. He became the hippie generation's poet laureate with such hits as "Mellow Yellow," "Sunshine Superman," "Wear Your Love Like Heaven," "Hurdy Gurdy Man," "Jennifer Juniper," and "Boo Boo Barabajagal," which featured a stinging guitar solo by master stringbender Jeff Beck.

3. FRED NEIL

A writer of several classic songs and a performer with a sterling reputation who was regarded in his time as a genius, Fred Neil is barely remembered today.

If he is recalled, it's because he wrote "Everybody's Talkin'," which Harry Nilsson took to the top of the charts in 1969. But Neil, who passed away in 2001 after 30 years out of the spotlight, also had his song, "Dolphins," a paean to his favorite mammals, recorded by British rock/folkie Billy Bragg.

Neil was primarily folk-influenced, but he also worked jazz and Indian music into his songs. He was uncompromising and often difficult to work with, but others loved to play with him. Buzzy

Linhart, '70s folk/rocker, was a sideman of his, playing vibraphone. Jim Hendrix was also a friend. John Sebastian of the Lovin' Spoonful served as one of Neil's sessionmen.

Faced with the possibility of mainstream success, Neil turned his back on the music industry in the late '60s and retired to Coconut Grove, Florida, where he spent time relaxing, swimming, and studying his beloved dolphins.

4. DAVID BOWIE

The Thin White Duke a "new Dylan"? Strange but true. One of Bowie's early guises, back in the late '60s, was as a folk-influenced singer/songwriter with a gift for wordplay and theatrical presentation.

It was this Bowie who wrote and sang "Space Oddity," "Memories of a Free Festival," and "The Man Who Sold the World." Of course, this phase—certainly more hippie than Dylan ever got—didn't last long; Bowie grew more theatrical and less folky, giving birth to his *Hunky Dory* and *Aladdin Sane* personas and, in 1973, to Ziggy Stardust.

But like Dylan, Bowie has maintained an artistic vision and a loyal fan base that has stayed with him through good albums and bad. And, as with Dylan, there have been plenty of both.

5. BRUCE SPRINGSTEEN

Perhaps the only man ever to truly survive the "new Dylan" tag, Bruce Springsteen grew up playing the bars and clubs in Asbury Park, New Jersey. He was never thought of as an early Dylan, but rather as a '70s successor to the mid-'60s model.

By the early '70s, much of the urgency had seeped from rock music, with the scene dominated by floaty singer/songwriters, glam rock, and progressive noodling. Springsteen, signed to Columbia records in 1973, was a welcome sight and sound to rock fans and critics. Some of them tended to over-emote in their praise: Jon Landau wrote at the time, "I have seen the future of rock & roll, and it's called Bruce Springsteen."

Springsteen's much-anticipated third album, 1975's *Born to Run,* brought with it comparisons to Roy Orbison, Phil Spector, and, above all, Dylan for his world-weary tone, '60s-influenced song structures, and use of two keyboard players. The album and its title tune were deserved worldwide hits, and "The Boss," as Springsteen came to be known, has never looked back.

The Dylan comparisons remain valid. During his nearly 30-year career, Springsteen has recorded folk-influenced ballads, topical political songs, country tunes, and even an album, *The Ghost of Tom Joad,* based on episodes from Steinbeck's *The Grapes of Wrath.*

6. ELVIS COSTELLO

Literate, talented, and charismatic enough to be thought of as a "new Dylan," Declan Patrick MacManus (renamed Elvis Costello in 1978) was viewed as a successor to the Zimmerman throne for his witty wordplay, on which audiences hung, and his cool, tough-guy persona.

Signing to British new-wave record label Stiff in 1976, the Liverpool-born Costello looked the punk in his Buddy Holly glasses and thrift-store clothes, but his recent musical background included plenty of then-unfashionable music. On a series of demos recorded in 1975, he had sung Dylan's "Knockin' on Heaven's Door" as well as the Amazing Rhythm Aces' "Third-Rate Romance" and such straight country material as "Imagination Is a Powerful Deceiver." Not exactly leather and safety pins.

But just as Dylan went electric after hearing The Animals' "House of the Rising Sun," Costello heard the Sex Pistols and the Clash and began writing songs like "Watching the Detectives," "Less than Zero," "Big Tears," and "Welcome to the Working Week." Costello was not strictly punk, but he was exciting, intelligent, passionate, and totally "other," the way Dylan had been 10 years earlier.

7. STEVE FORBERT

In 1976, just 21 years old, the Mississippi-born Forbert went north to New York City, as Dylan had done more than 15 years earlier, and built a local following.

Forbert was ambitious, intelligent, and talented. After working night jobs and playing every club in the city that would have him, Forbert was signed by CBS. His first album, *Alive on Arrival,* gained critical and public attention. In 1980, a single from the *Jackrabbit Slim* LP, "Romeo's Tune," climbed all the way to #11 on the *Billboard* chart.

So what did Forbert get for his efforts? A tag as a "new Dylan," as do many rural youngsters who "go electric."

Of course, Forbert could never recover from this. His popularity plummeted as his new material, not quite as catchy or well-thought-out, couldn't find an audience. Sporadic comebacks have yet to return him to prominence, but Forbert still retains a fan base and releases records and tours.

8. BILLY BRAGG

Billy Bragg, blessed with a prominent nose and a thick, working-class British voice, was nobody's idea of a matinee idol. But possessing a socialist sensibility laced with wry humor and singing with surprising tenderness, Bragg galvanizes his audience as Dylan has.

Bragg was well known and loved by many for his embrace of labor unions and left-wing causes (he helped found the Red Wedge tour in the '80s) as well as for his no-B.S. love songs like "A New England," "The Milkman of Human Kindness," and "St. Swithin's Day." Like the early Dylan, he eventually became as comfortable singing about relationships as about corporate or governmental power.

By 1999, Bragg got around to collaborating with alt-country band Wilco in putting music to some "lost" words of one of Dylan's heroes: Woody Guthrie. On the resulting album, *Mermaid Avenue,* Bragg contributed some of his best melodic work and song settings, and his voice perfectly communicated Guthrie's homespun but often whacked-out lyrics.

9. TRACY CHAPMAN

Breaking onto the scene in 1988 with her "Fast Car" single and self-titled first album, Tracy Chapman—a black woman trained in African studies at Tufts University—became an unlikely "next Dylan."

Blending the personal and political, often in the same song, Chapman's folk and blues-based music was rich, passionate, and urgent. She sang at a Nelson Mandela birthday tribute in London in 1988 and shortly thereafter broke into the British charts.

However, she was unable to maintain her early momentum. Her second album, 1989's *Crossroads,* was seen as an artistic and commercial letdown. She did not truly reemerge until her fourth album, 1995's *New Beginning,* which featured an old Chapman composition dressed up and rocked out for the singles market. "Give Me One Reason" made the Top 10.

10. JOHN WESLEY HARDING

He had this one coming. Anyone wanting to avoid a "new Dylan" tag would be advised to avoid naming himself after one of Dylan's albums.

Born Wesley Harding Stace in Sussex, England, in 1965, he changed his name in the late '80s while at Cambridge University. After one album, 1988's *It Happened One Night,* he was signed by Sire and released several more albums. The first, *Here Comes the Groom,* was recorded with the backing band of another onetime "new Dylan," Elvis Costello.

Harding has never made the leap to stardom, but he has moved to America, continues to tour and record, and has a loyal following.

What Is This Music?

Guitar, bass, piano, and drums have formed the basis of rock bands from the very beginning. Usually, a band can throw a saxophone, an organ, or maybe a steel guitar in without attracting a glance, but when you get into instruments like oud, saz, sitar, simran horn, hurdy-gurdy, and clarinet . . .

1. GARY LEWIS & THE PLAYBOYS

The son of film comedian Jerry Lewis was a big star from 1965 through 1968, scoring ten Top 10 hits. He did this despite a voice best described as shaky and a band that featured a honking accordion—not an instrument well equipped to deal with mid-'60s rock compositions.

The Playboys usually were replaced on recordings by top sessionmen like Leon Russell and Al Kooper. Then again, that might not have been so bad for future generations; listening to the original band's version of the Kinks' "All Day and All of the Night" on the first Playboys album isn't one of rock's great experiences.

2. 13TH FLOOR ELEVATORS

Five Texas acidheads who somehow stumbled to the outer edges of stardom (their bizarre 1966 appearance on Dick Clark's *Where the Action Is!* TV show is one of the true highlights of '60s rock), the Elevators were among the first groups to publicly promote the psychedelic experience.

An odd combination of British-influenced rock, electric folk, country, and LSD-influenced ravings, the Elevators sounded like no other band. Featuring lyricist/jug player (!) Tommy Hall (responsible in large part for the group's druggy ambience) and singer/songwriter Roky Erickson, who has spent much of the last 30 years in and out of mental institutions, the Elevators recorded many memorable songs, such as "You're Gonna Miss Me," "Reverberation (Doubt)," and "Fluctuation."

Drug busts and emotional problems almost inevitably brought the Elevators crashing down, but they are still remembered. A 13th Floor Elevators tribute album, *Where the Pyramid Meets the Eye,* featured artists like R.E.M., ZZ Top, and

Julian Cope performing Erickson's songs, but somehow the jug was left out of the equation.

3. KALEIDOSCOPE

A five-man mid-'60s band from California, Kaleidoscope (not to be confused with a U.K. psychedelic outfit of the same era) used versatility and experimentation as its calling cards. David Lindley, later a much-in-demand L.A. session-man, and Chris Darrow, who would craft records by artists ranging in style from folk to punk, are the most well-known alumnae of the group.

Fusing everything from the then-in-vogue psychedelic rock improvisations to jazz, blues, Arabic music, country, folk, and even Latin rhythms, Kaleidoscope played not only guitars, bass, and drums, but also made use of such diverse instruments as mandolin, oud (an Eastern stringed instrument resembling an overgrown egg with a stick strapped to it), banjo, organ, clarinet, saz (a guitar-like drone instrument), violin, and all manner of keyboards.

Predictably, such an eclectic mix of music made it hard to pinpoint Kaleidoscope commercially, and despite several well-received albums, they never could produce a hit. The mix of personalities in the band was also volatile; Darrow didn't stick around for long, and Lindley was reputedly difficult to work with.

However, in their original guise, Kaleidoscope influenced bands ranging from Led Zeppelin to Camper Van Beethoven, and returned to record again sporadically in the '70s, '80s, and '90s.

4. CAPTAIN BEEFHEART AND THE MAGIC BAND

Don Van Vliet, alias Captain Beefheart, recorded a dozen cult albums in the '60s and '70s, often featuring obscure or even handmade instruments to help flesh out his unique blend of avant-garde jazz, Delta blues, and beat poetry.

His classic *Trout Mask Replica* LP featured a band member who played only bass clarinet. Over the years, Beefheart played odd wind instruments such as the musette and simran horn and sometimes used the technique (borrowed from free-jazz innovator Rahsaan Roland Kirk) of playing two saxophones simultaneously.

While Beefheart didn't always stay quite that far out, he was never "conventional." He continued to rename his band members with outrageous appellations like Winged Eel Fingerling, Zoot Horn Rollo, and Rockette Morton, and to make use of self-titled instruments like "flesh horn" and "steel-appendage guitar."

5. **JETHRO TULL**

A British blues-influenced combo with a flute-playing frontman? Only in the '60s. Traffic and Love had used flute earlier, but the 1968 emergence of Jethro Tull was different.

Flutist Ian Anderson was the acknowledged leader of the band, originally named in honor of a 19th-century English farmer. Delivering blues and jazz-inflected melodies over a driving rock beat, and adding odd lyrics often concerned with death, insanity, and the disconnected relationships of modern society, Anderson and the band became huge stars, especially in the United States.

The band had some hit singles, including "Living in the Past," "Locomotive Breath," and "Bungle in the Jungle," but they were better known for their concept albums such as *Thick as a Brick* and *A Passion Play*. The Tull are still playing, and Anderson remains a singular figure.

6. **SILVER APPLES**

Drums and synthesized keyboard sounds. Sounds pretty '90s, doesn't it? But Silver Apples did it in the late '60s.

Two members of a New York R&B combo, the Overland Stage Electric Band, drummer Dan Taylor and singer Simeon Coxe, wanted to play more outré music. Exit the two.

As leader of Jethro Tull, Ian Anderson has fashioned a singular
presence that has endured for three decades.

Simeon was a painter by trade who later discovered folk music. Always adventurous, in early 1967 he found an old oscillator, a huge table full of dials and knobs that could be "played" to produce odd sounds. He and Taylor decided to form a duo. Simeon modified the oscillator, which Taylor nicknamed a "Simeon," and played it by constantly adjusting knobs with his hands to build melodies and playing foot pedals to construct bass notes. He sang, though usually in an off-key warble, and overdubbed other instruments on the band's recordings.

After some early high-profile New York City gigs in 1968, the Apples were signed by Kapp, a label more well known for soft rock and folk. Their first album, *Silver Apples,* was a feast of bleeps, blurts, and syncopated drum parts. It included "Seagreen Serenade," on which Simeon tootled on a recorder, and "Oscillations," the closest thing to a hit single they could produce. Their second LP, *Contact,* emerged the next year. The odd "A Pox on You," a highlight, even featured Simeon plucking away at a banjo.

The group did not last. Taylor departed (he has been MIA for 30 years) with Simeon remaining underground until other acts, such as Stereolab, Big Black, and Atari Teenage Riot began to sing his praises in the '90s. Even though the original Simeon oscillator is probably at the bottom of a junk pile, Coxe reformed Silver Apples again in 1998.

7. **SAILOR**

Guitarist/singer/painter Georg Kajanus, much more of an artist and showman than a rocker, formed this four-piece group in France in 1974. The band featured an accordionist/mandolin player, a drummer, and a bassist. Sailor's sound was also defined by a custom-built "nickelodeon," a double-sided keyboard that sounded something like a carnival hurdy-gurdy. It took two men to play the contraption.

To make things even stranger, the band dressed in sailor suits. Their sound, originally written to be expressed in a musical theater idiom, emerged from a universe seemingly inhabited by traditional Eastern European musicians attempting to play Roxy Music songs on Broadway.

Their early music was more popular in the rest of Europe than in England, but a Roxy-esque (think "Virginia Plain") song, "Glass of Champagne," provided Sailor with a British hit in 1975. Another hit single, "Girls Girls Girls," followed, but the band couldn't capitalize on their success and, understandably, never broke through in America. The

Sailor concept continued on and off until 1995, when Kajanus left for good.

British popsters Supergrass covered "Glass of Champagne" in their stage shows during 2000. Just goes to show that *everything* comes back.

8. THE MEKONS

From punk to country, from rockabilly to flat-out rock & roll, the Mekons have done almost everything you can do in a 25-year career.

Starting as a Clash-inflected punk band in 1976 (who nonetheless made fun of the Clash's "White Riot" with their own "Never Been in a Riot"), the Mekons—guitarist Jon Langford and singer Tom Greenhalgh are the only remaining originals—quickly expanded their universe.

Always a disorganized, ad hoc aggregation, the band at various times has included accordion, acoustic guitar, oud, and violin as well as more traditional rock instruments. The Mekons took on all comers in what became a signature style: intense, often sloppy music played with great verve and wit. Their live shows are some of the best (and funniest) any group can offer.

Seemingly on the fringes of mainstream success with early '90s albums like *The Mekons Rock & Roll* and *Curse of the Mekons,* the band never quite broke through, but they continue to

James A. Newberry

The unpredictable Mekons, one of rock's great live acts.

record and play live. Langford, a painter, also has side projects like the Pine Valley Cosmonauts, Waco Brothers, and Skull Orchard, while charming second singer Sally Timms records solo.

9. CHUMBAWAMBA

Punk and trumpet came together on the ultra-catchy 1997 single by Chumbawamba, "Tubthumping."

The band began as a hardcore punk three-piece in England in 1982. Committed to anarchist causes and interested in combining different genres of music, "Chumba" grew in number as well as artistically and even ended up signing with a major record label in 1997 (receiving a pillorying from the alternative press as a result). At last count, they have released 11 albums and two dozen singles and EPs.

The now eight-piece Chumbawamba have placed some of their songs in movies, but have rejected other opportunities and have turned large advertising commissions down flat. During an appearance on ABC's daytime talk show *The View*, Chumbawamba punctuated "Tubthumping" with cries of "Free Mumia" in honor of imprisoned African-American activist Mumia Abu-Jamal.

As they define themselves, Chumba are "Punk. Always. Not punk rock—punk. Thus we can encompass folk, doo-wop, a capella, techno, trip-hop, pop, emo . . ."

10. CAMPER VAN BEETHOVEN

CVB, five (or six, depending on who showed up) northern California smart alecks who came from punk and ska backgrounds, also had deep affinity for '60s psychedelia, varied ethnic music, old-time country, and even '70s progressive rock.

The resulting mix of tastes and personalities coalesced into Camper Van Beethoven. Their first LP, 1984's *Telephone Free Landslide Victory*, boasted a catchy chunk of surrealistic rock, "Take the Skinheads Bowling," and resulting albums got even weirder as Camper expanded their sound to include a baffling menu of styles.

Chief songwriter David Lowery, later frontman of Cracker, proved a witty observer of California culture as well as an appealing singer. The band (featuring hot guitarist Greg Lisher and the versatile Jonathan Segal on violin, sitar, and keyboards) came at music from several different angles at once, which always kept things interesting. Their five albums, and a bagful of tunes released only later in compilations, have cemented Camper's reputation.

Music Lovers

Music makes strange bedfellows. Or is it that bedfellows make strange music? Plenty of groups have tried to combine music and romance, with a few making it a permanent arrangement.

1. SONNY AND CHER

Sonny and Cher were the first famous hippie couple.

When the two met (and were married) in Los Angeles in 1964, Sonny Bono was 29 and Cherilyn Sarkisian La Piere was 18. Bono was an aggressive young turk in the Phil Spector mold, a songwriter and producer on the make; the fetching Sarkisian had appeared as a backup vocalist on the Crystals' epochal hit, "Da Doo Ron Ron."

They began making records together, one of which, "I Got You, Babe," was a worldwide #1 in 1965. The two then enjoyed 12 more Top 40 hits, recording together and solo, through 1967. They were camera-friendly and very hip: Cher made halter tops fashionable, and Sonny helped do the same for wild print shirts.

After their fall from the charts, variety TV beckoned, and their hugely popular *Sonny & Cher Comedy Hour* ran for three years on CBS. Their easy manner and obvious love for each other made them a favorite of the American public, and their little girl, Chastity, was a part of the proceedings as well. Long after their marriage broke up in 1974, Sonny and Cher would still sing "I Got You, Babe" on special occasions.

Sonny Bono later represented California in the U.S. Congress before dying in a 1998 ski accident. Cher, who had relationships with other musicians, such as Gregg Allman, Gene Simmons of Kiss, and Richie Sambora of Bon Jovi, continues to act and sing. She enjoyed a massive comeback in 1999 with the hit "Believe."

2. THE MAMAS AND THE PAPAS

Folk singers John and Michelle Phillips, married in 1962 (John had been married to someone else when the two met), joined up the next year with Canadian singer Denny Doherty and Baltimore-born "Mama Cass" Elliott to form the Mamas and the Papas.

After some time singing and hanging around in New York and in the Virgin Islands, the foursome relocated to Los Angeles.

The ride began once Phillips's haunting "California Dreamin'" was released to universal acclaim in late 1965. For two years, the Mamas and the Papas were one of the most popular acts in the world. The band had eight Top 20 hits in 18 months, including "Monday, Monday," "Words of Love," "Dedicated to the One I Love," and "Creeque Alley."

While things were going great guns on the charts, Michelle and John's marriage was crumbling. Michelle had been in a protracted affair with Doherty since the early days of the group. In fact, one of the Mamas and the Papas' top hits, "I Saw Her Again (Last Night)" (written by John Phillips for Doherty to sing), painfully addressed the adulterous relationship. To exacerbate the heart-rending sexual politics of the band, Doherty was also the apple of Cass Elliott's eye; her marriage had ended recently.

Heavy recording and touring, excessive drugs and alcohol, and overwhelming emotional tension eventually broke up the "family" by 1968. None of the four enjoyed substantial solo success, and it took years for each of them to rebuild their personal and professional lives.

3. **VELVET UNDERGROUND**

When Manhattanites Lou Reed, John Cale, and Sterling Morrison recruited drummer Maureen Tucker in 1965 to play their out-of-whack blend of rock music, they were already street smart. But they had no idea of the special New York brand of insanity that awaited them.

Hooking up with artist and social gadfly Andy Warhol, the foursome were sucked into the bizarre lineup of personalities and hangers-on at Warhol's Factory studio. Cale almost immediately became involved with doomed actress Edie Sedgwick, while the already streetwise Reed and singer Nico (Christa Päffgen), who also was asked to join the band, linked up as sexual partners.

While the two weren't really meant to be together, Reed wrote two truly beautiful songs for Nico to sing: "Femme Fatale" and "I'll Be Your Mirror." He and bandmates Morrison and Cale also contributed to Nico's first solo album, *Chelsea Girls*. Nico, a fascinating figure in her own right, was also involved with musicians like Bob Dylan and Jackson Browne.

Reed also acted out his nascent gay impulses, and most members of VU experimented with amphetamines and heroin. Sex partners came and went, and the rotation of drugs, sex, paranoia, aggression, touring, and social misfit status shaped the group's songwriting and playing. A lovely place to visit, but a hard place to live.

4. JEFFERSON AIRPLANE/STARSHIP

Grace Slick and her brother, Darby, played in The Great Society, a mid-'60s San Francisco band. When Grace departed, she took two songs with her: "White Rabbit" and "Somebody to Love." They would become hits for the next band she'd join, Jefferson Airplane.

The Airplane, a six-piece folk-rock act, lost singer Signe Toly to motherhood in 1966 and quickly recruited Slick. She and Marty Balin brought outstanding voices to the party, while Paul Kantner and Jorma Kaukonen provided the band with two distinctive guitar stylists. *Surrealistic Pillow,* the first album with Slick, still rates as one of the best American '60s rock LPs.

Romance played a big part in the band's history. Slick originally paired off with drummer Spencer Dryden, but eventually she and Kantner set up shop. Their alliance helped push Balin from prominence, then into the background, and finally out of the group. Numerous changes in personnel over the years led to varying sounds and varying degrees of success.

Slick and Kantner remained together until 1984, by which point the band had been renamed

Jefferson Starship to reflect musical changes. Balin came back to the fold and then left again, responding with disgust when asked whether he had been a partner of Slick's ("I wouldn't let Grace Slick blow me").

In 1990, the *Surrealistic Pillow* Airplane, minus Dryden, reunited. It's not known who slept where.

5. FLEETWOOD MAC

The original '60s iteration of Fleetwood Mac was as unglamorous a combo as could be imagined. Guitarists Peter Green and Jeremy Spencer, drummer Mick Fleetwood, and bassist John McVie took great pains to dress drably, putting their British blues-rock fusion front and center.

Green and Spencer eventually turned to religion and away from music. By the early '70s, Fleetwood Mac included keyboardist Christine Perfect, who eventually married McVie and wrote some of her most tender songs about him.

In 1974, the Mac was at its lowest ebb. Guitarist Bob Welch, in the band for four years, had departed. Fleetwood recalled a 1973 album made by California couple Lindsey Buckingham and Stevie Nicks, and figured that the pair would be a good if somewhat bizarre addition to the remaining three group members.

The new Mac rode their three-singer/songwriter lineup to massive success with three huge albums:

1975's *Fleetwood Mac,* 1977's *Rumours,* and 1979's *Tusk.* The public became fascinated with the members of the good-looking and talented band, all of whom enjoyed swirling, out-of-control personal lives that served as fodder for a hungry rock press.

It's fascinating that the group's biggest success, *Rumours,* came in the wake of the disintegration of both interband relationships. "Second Hand News" and "Go Your Own Way" were Buckingham's kiss-offs to Nicks, who wrote the aching but defiant "Silver Spring" and "Dreams," in turn, about her ex. The McVies were also coming apart at the seams, with Christine taking up with former Beach Boy Dennis Wilson. Finally, Mick Fleetwood nursed a long-standing unrequited crush on Stevie Nicks.

"Sara," one of Stevie Nicks's greatest songs, was written ostensibly about Fleetwood's wife. Actually, according to Nicks, it was a story about the band's interpersonal relationships.

6. INCREDIBLE STRING BAND

Welshmen Mike Heron, Robin Williamson, and Clive Palmer came together in mid-'60s Britain to play folk and traditional music. They formed the Incredible String Band, a name influenced both by the anything-goes mid-'60s and the three musicians' collective ability to master seemingly every existing stringed instrument.

After one album, the more traditional-minded Palmer departed, perhaps sensing what was to come. Meanwhile, Williamson and girlfriend Licorice McKechnie went to Morocco, returning fully psychedelicized. Heron became involved with mountain climber Rose Simpson, and the four were soon musically as well as sexually compatible; the Incredibles' folk/world/psych fusion soon established them as Britain's foremost hippie act.

By the band's third LP, the celebrated *Hangman's Beautiful Daughter* (1968), Licorice was singing and tapping at various percussion instruments. Rose was soon brought into the band to sing, and the four (along with various friends) moved into a Welsh commune, where bed-hopping and habitual dope-smoking were de rigueur. They even appeared, not so successfully, at Woodstock.

Eventually, Rose departed, relationships became strained, the commune shut down, and the ISB became more high-tech and commercial. The magic was lost, and by 1974, Heron and Williamson couldn't stand to work together.

A 2000 reunion included the three original males, but lacked Simpson, by now a mayoress of a Welsh village, and McKechnie, who disappeared during the '70s.

7. DELANEY & BONNIE

Two young singers, Delaney Bramlett and Bonnie Lynn, had been treading the boards in different locales—Delaney as a sessionman in California and Bonnie as one of Ike Turner's Ikettes in Memphis—when they met and quickly married in 1967.

Finding they shared a common love of soul, gospel, and country music, the two formed a loose group of friends, including Leon Russell, Bobby Whitlock, Rita Coolidge, and Carl Radle, to back them at gigs and recordings. They, and others, helped on the 1969 *Accept No Substitute: The Original Delaney and Bonnie* album, which instantly propelled the act into the rock elite.

By later that year, the loose "group" had caught the ears of Eric Clapton and George Harrison across the ocean. Wishing to escape their depressing band situations (Clapton with Cream and Blind Faith, Harrison with the Beatles), the two made overtures to the Americans. As a result, Clapton's 1970 hit single, "After Midnight," featured D&B, while keyboardsman Bobby Whitlock appeared on Harrison's *All Things Must Pass*.

However, due to the onset of hard drugs, the pressures of touring, and heavy work schedules, the "friends" soon broke up, with three joining

Clapton and some touring with The Rolling Stones. Russell concentrated on solo work. Delaney and Bonnie made three more albums, each meeting with decreasing success, before busting up the marriage and the act in 1973.

8. HEART

Ann and Nancy Wilson grew up in Washington during the late sixties wanting to play rock music. Despite the fact that few women at the time strapped on the equipment, the sisters were undeterred, learning to sing and master several instruments each.

Ann, three years older, eventually hooked up with local musicians Steve Fossen, Mike Flicker, and Roger Fisher, who had been bandmates for years, most recently with a group called Heart.

On joining the band, Ann began a relationship with Mike Flicker. When Nancy came aboard a bit later, she set up shop with Roger Fisher. A short time later, the band uprooted and moved to Canada, largely to help Fisher avoid the draft.

The musically and sexually attuned group's first album, *Dreamboat Annie,* was released in 1974. Featuring mostly Ann Wilson's compositions, *Annie* was a well-deserved major hit. At this point, Flicker left the band to concentrate on audio engineering.

By 1978, Heart were an established and popular act, having released hit albums, *Little Queen* and *Dog and Butterfly*. But that year, both Wilson sisters ended their relationships. Fisher departed Heart.

The band enjoyed a new wave of success in the 1980s, refashioning themselves as high-tech hitmakers and MTV video stars. As the millennium rolled around, Nancy Wilson married film director Cameron Crowe, which assured her a prime piece of the soundtrack action when Crowe made his '70s-homage rock film, *Almost Famous*.

9. EURYTHMICS

Annie Lennox and Dave Stewart met in a restaurant in the mid-'70s where Lennox, a classically trained flutist, was a waitress. Stewart proposed to her immediately, and while they didn't wed that instant, they began musical and romantic partnerships and before long were joined in matrimony.

The duo's second band, the Tourists, scored a hit with a remake of Dusty Springfield's "I Only Want to Be with You." However, further success eluded them, and the band imploded in 1980, taking Stewart and Lennox's relationship down the tubes with it.

But, oddly enough, they wanted to still work together. Their second project would be titled

Eurythmics. Their 1982 *Sweet Dreams* album was a worldwide hit—the title track one of the most memorable records of the era.

From there, the two made eight successful albums and enjoyed more than a dozen U.K. hit singles, playing in styles ranging from dreamy synth-pop and Eastern-influenced soundscapes to all-out rock and '60s-styled soul before choosing solo careers in 1991.

How do two independent, headstrong people formerly in a four-year relationship work together so closely? Lennox told Robert Hilburn in 1986, "I wanted to break away from that [relationship], but I also knew creatively I didn't want to work with anybody else except Dave.

"There was this strange tension—the pain of the breakup and the excitement of working together on the music. In some ways, that tension has never really gone away."

10. DEE-LITE

One of the first hip-hop-influenced collectives to achieve major pop success, the multicultural groove collective Dee-Lite rode wild samples of '60s and '70s music, trendy beats, and kitschy charm to early '90s stardom.

"Lady Miss Kier" Kirby, a New York City gad-fly, hooked up with two DJs, Russian emigré

Dmitry Brill and Japanese native Towa Tei, in the late '80s to create a fun, entertaining fusion of current dance grooves, psychedelic production values, and a relentlessly positive approach. They wore wild, retro clothes, made funny videos, and quickly became stars.

"Groove Is in the Heart," featuring a sample from Herbie Hancock's "Bring Down the Birds," a rap from A Tribe Called Quest's Q-Tip, and vocal interjections from former Parliament/Funkadelic bassist Bootsy Collins, was a radio and club hit in 1990. Their first LP, *World Clique,* was a joyful mix of house music, solid hooks, and what the band called "sampla-delic" production.

Kirby and Brill were married for much of the band's tenure, which included two more (less successful) releases and a compilation/rarities CD. However, the couple broke up before the third LP, and Towa Tei was replaced by another DJ, Ani, in 1994. Dee-Lite flickered out for good soon after.

You're No Good

The definition of "artistic integrity" has certainly changed in pop music. Back in the '60s and '70s, even the biggest and best groups were often augmented by session musicians. (For instance, few people know that '60s balladeer Gene Pitney played piano on some early '60s Rolling Stones sessions. *Gene Pitney??*)

Today, with sampling, ever-more-sophisticated studio techniques, and synthesizers, it's hard to tell who's playing what. And fewer and fewer people seem to care.

1. THE BEATLES

Yes, even the Fabs weren't good enough, at least at first.

For the group's initial recording on the Parlophone label in 1962, "Love Me Do," producer George Martin replaced Ringo Starr with session drummer Andy White. Starr had joined the band just recently, and Martin wanted to make sure he was covered just in case the unproven Ringo couldn't hack it.

Two versions of the song were produced, one featuring White's very wooden drum work, with Starr banging a tambourine (which became the 45 version), and one in which Starr himself was allowed to man the drums (this version was released on the group's first album).

2. **HERMAN'S HERMITS**

When the British band, led by toothy 15-year-old Peter Noone, hooked up with British producer Mickie Most, they scored more than a dozen major American hits.

Unfortunately, the band—a tight little R&B group with some talent, especially considering they were mostly in their teens—eventually lost the ability to record their own backing tracks. (They are playing, however, on "I'm Henry the Eighth, I Am," "I'm into Something Good," and "Mrs. Brown, You've Got a Lovely Daughter.")

Mickie Most didn't allow most of the group to play, although lead guitarist Derek "Lek" Lekenby was sometimes good enough to pass muster.

The group did plenty of world tours and a film *(Hold On!)*, but never established themselves as a "serious" band due to Most's particular brand of commercial instinct, which turned them into solely a teenybop act. By the time the ultraserious year, 1967, rolled around, the Hermits were viewed as irrelevant.

3. **THE BYRDS**

Their credentials as a rock band wafer-thin, the Byrds cut "Mr. Tambourine Man" and "I Knew I'd Want You" in 1964 with only lead guitarist Roger McGuinn allowed to play his instrument.

McGuinn, who picked at his 12-string guitar and sang lead on "Tambourine," was augmented by a trio of L.A. session musicians. David Crosby and Gene Clark were allowed to provide backup vocals, while the rhythm section (drummer Mike Clarke and bassist Chris Hillman) was left to watch.

By the following year, when "Mr. Tambourine Man" was released on Columbia and became a big hit, the band had become much more competent (especially Hillman, a bluegrass mandolin player by trade who eventually evolved into a top-flight bass guitarist) and, from that point on, recorded their own backings.

4. **THE BEACH BOYS**

When Brian Wilson stopped touring with the Beach Boys in 1965, and began writing more complex songs, he decided it would be a good idea to record backing tracks for the band's records with top session musicians while the other Boys were on the road.

This was probably just as well; while lead guitarist Carl Wilson was an undeniably gifted and inventive musician, the other BBs weren't really up to Brian's far more sophisticated tempos and instrumental parts. Brian even allowed other bass guitarists, such as Carol Kaye, to take over what had been his instrumental role.

Most of the landmark *Beach Boys Today!* and *Pet Sounds* LPs from 1965–66 were cut with session musicians (with Kaye replacing Brian on many songs). Even the less complex *20/20* LP (1969), for example, featured assistance from touring-band guitarist Ed Carter.

5. THE MONKEES

The Monkees' first two albums were recorded almost entirely by session musicians. But a little-known fact about the "band" is that Mike Nesmith, Peter Tork, Micky Dolenz, and Davy Jones were originally given the opportunity to record their own music.

All four had musical backgrounds before being signed to play a band in an NBC-TV series. Nesmith was a promising country/folk guitarist and

Clark Besch

Three of the Monkees—*from left,* Peter Tork, Davy Jones, and Mickey Dolenz—on tour in the 1990s.

singer, while Tork, a veteran of the folk coffee-house circuit, could play guitar, bass, banjo, and all types of keyboards. Dolenz played guitar in an L.A. band and showed aptitude for drumming when asked. Jones, a show-tunes-and-soul music-besotted singer, had released an album in 1965.

More than 20 years after the band's breakup, a track apparently recorded by the four in early 1966, "Of You," was released for the first time on a compilation, called *Missing Links.* The song, a

Ricky Nelson-style number, was played compe-
tently enough, but lacked the commercial drive
that *über*-hitmaker Don Kirshner brought to the
table when asked by the show's producers to
punch things up some months later.

Following the band's blow-up with Kirshner in
early 1967, the Monkees had more control over
their own music, recording the *Headquarters* album
as a unit. After this, though, they only played
together for a few more weeks before separating
into separate camps to cut their own material with
their own friends.

6. LOVE

One of the truly quintessential L.A. '60s bands,
Love made two acclaimed albums *(Love* and *Da
Capo)* in 1965–66. For their third album, guitarists/
songwriters Arthur Lee and Bryan MacLean constructed a beautiful suite of songs calling mainly
for acoustic, rather than electric, instrumentation.

But the rest of the five-man band, drugged out
and lazily unwilling to tour, couldn't hack the new
tunes. Producer Bruce Botnick called on session
musicians, including Neil Young, Don Randi, and
Billy Strange, to handle Lee's complex composition, "The Daily Planet." The sessioneers cut the
track with Lee and MacLean while the rest of the
band sat and watched.

This action caused the other three band members (drummer Michael Stuart, bassist Ken Forssi, and guitarist John Echols) such emotional trauma—tears and arguments ensued—that the fivesome actually pulled together and became a band again, recording the rest of the now-classic LP, *Forever Changes.*

7. STEELY DAN

Never a textbook rock band, Steely Dan began as a songwriting project for Donald Fagen and Walter Becker, two New York jazz/pop fans who, bored with writing songs for MOR artists and playing backup for Jay and the Americans, journeyed to California in 1971.

When ABC producer Steve Katz decided in 1972 that the duo should record some of their songs, Becker and Fagen sent for guitarist Denny Dias. Drummer Jim Hodder, singer David Palmer, and guitarist Jeff "Skunk" Baxter joined shortly thereafter.

After the band's first LP, the hit, *Can't Buy a Thrill,* Palmer was fired. By the third album, *Pretzel Logic,* Hodder had been replaced by two session drummers, even though he was still pictured on the sleeve. He drifted away, and Baxter was soon axed (leaving him free to join the Doobie Brothers).

The band's fourth LP, 1975's *Katy Lied,* was the last to feature Dias in a major role. There was no longer a true Steely Dan; Becker and Fagen from then on simply brought in whatever session-men they wanted to provide a certain sound on a certain song.

8. EDIE BRICKELL & THE NEW BOHEMIANS

Perhaps they were in over their heads, but Edie Brickell and the New Bohemians, a jammin' bunch from Austin, Texas, got a quick whiff of just how cruel the rock business can be.

Signed by Geffen Records in 1986 after an impressive demo tape and some solid shows, the New Bohemians were assigned to producer Pat Moran, who almost immediately fired drummer Brandon Aly. This threw the band into an emotional tailspin that even a hit album *(Shooting Rubberbands at the Stars)* and single ("What I Am") couldn't stop.

Splitting into band-against-Brickell factions (the musicians thought the singer was on a star trip), they broke up while the record was climbing the charts. Even though Brickell came back shortly after to do a tour, the band's chemistry had been damaged; they split after just one more album.

9. THE RUNAWAYS

The first significant all-girl rock band, the Runaways—a five-piece group featuring guitarists Joan Jett and Lita Ford as well as jailbait singer Cherie Currie—came to prominence in California in 1975. "Cherry Bomb" was their first song to gain notice, for both its overt sexuality and its rock-solid rhythm and tough feel.

Initial bassist Michael Steele, who resurfaced in 1983 as part of the Bangles, departed, and her replacement, Jackie Fox, wasn't allowed to record. She told *Mojo* magazine in 2000, "The story that I wasn't allowed to play on the album is true . . . if that wasn't bad enough, I'd actually get calls telling me to come down to the studio to show Nigel Harrison my bass parts!" Harrison would later join Blondie.

The band's man in charge, legendary Svengali/near-dictator Kim Fowley, stopped at nothing in an attempt to get "his girls" to the top. His endless, brutal verbal tirades against the ladies' egos were intended, he said, to make them tougher, but only engendered enmity.

Jett, a hard-rockin' popster, and Ford, a prototypical metal mama, became solo stars in the '80s, while the Runaways' approach lived on in groups like the Go-Gos, the Donnas, and Elastica.

10. MILLI VANILLI

It's one thing to have outside musicians play on your songs. But outside *singers?* Pretending to be *you?*

The duo of Frenchman Fabrice Morvan and German Rob Pilatus, titled Milli Vanilli by longtime dance producer Frank Farian, released an album in 1988 *(Girl, You Know It's True)* that spawned five nearly identical-sounding hit singles. Three of them—"Baby, Don't Forget My Number," "Girl, I'm Gonna Miss You," and "Blame It on the Rain"—reached #1.

The handsome, sculpted model-types were the toast of the music industry, at least until it was revealed in 1990 (though it had already been an open industry secret) that neither Morvan nor Pilatus had actually sung any of the songs. The actual vocalists were John Davis, Brad Howe, and Charles Shaw.

The Grammy Award the duo was awarded the year before was taken away, and Milli Vanilli was essentially finished. It got worse: Pilatus, who attempted suicide in 1991, died in 1998 of a drug-and-alcohol overdose.

Oops! Wrong Haircut

Rock music has always been about more than just the songs; appearance is critical. Even if not conventionally beautiful, an entertainer can still be attractive and influential: plenty of great bands and singers have changed the way we think about our looks.

1. ELVIS PRESLEY

In 1956, Elvis Presley's DA haircut, slicked back and shaped but still unkempt and dangerous, was just one of the more outrageous things about him. His clothes, his wiggling hips, his fusion of country and blues, and his thick Southern accent also terrified the bluenoses and Legion of Decency denizens of American society.

In addition, there may be no better rock & roll haircut than the one Elvis sported during his

1968–69 comeback. Early in his career, his hair was short but wild on top; later, he had long, shaped sideburns, a perfect melding of his classic style and the longer hairstyles of the late '60s. He still looked like a rebel, even as he became a Vegas mainstay and "all-around entertainer" who cozied up to Richard Nixon in the early '70s.

2. THE BEATLES

When the band first became popular in Britain in 1963, their hair was very long for the time. The group's so-hip Pierre Cardin collarless suits became a fashion trend, and, by 1964, when America caught Beatlemania, young men all over the world considered letting their hair grow out. Thanks to the Beatles, American men completely changed the way they thought of their appearance. Even old men bought Beatle wigs as party jokes.

Nearly every rock group of the time began growing their hair in Beatles pageboy cuts, and groups in the United States and Britain let their tresses grow to outrageous lengths. By 1969, all four had very, very long 'dos, especially John Lennon and George Harrison. When Lennon chopped off his hair both in 1966 (for a film) and in 1970 (as a political statement) it was news, just like everything else the Fab Four did.

3. **THE MONKS**

Five American servicemen stationed in Germany formed the Torquays in 1964, then renamed themselves the Monks in 1965. They were a band of outsiders: away from home, uncomfortable with their country's involvement in Vietnam, and misfits in the growing psychedelic and flower-power scenes.

Their music was a coarse, raw, R&B-inflected thump, played with guitar, bass, drums, organ, and amplified banjo (!). The Monks' hair and clothing were even stranger. The band wore black, with white rope (rather than neckties) knotted around their collars. Finally, they shaved their hair into monks' tonsures, bald on top and short at the back, sides, and front.

While it's not clear that the Monks' hair and clothes were inspirations—even now, few know much about the band—they certainly were revolutionary. When the band reformed for the New York City Cavestomp festival in 1999, the tonsures were mostly gone, but the friendships, black clothes, and pile-driving R&B were intact.

4. **LaBELLE**

Patti LaBelle and the Blue Belles had some success in the '60s, including the hit, "I Sold My

Heart to the Junkman." By 1970, they were struggling on the supper-club circuit before meeting Vicki Wickham, a British entrepreneur and former TV producer working for Buddah Records.

Wickham decided that Blue Belle Nona Hendryx should become the group's chief songwriter. Hendryx penned hard-edged, futuristic R&B, and to complete the concept, the group donned spacesuits and outrageous hairdos, complete with interwoven headpieces and peacock feathers.

Looking and sounding unlike anyone else, the newly christened LaBelle found an audience. In 1974, their album, *Nightbirds,* recorded with legendary pianist Allen Toussaint, yielded "Lady Marmalade," a classic slice of New Orleans-style funk that was the victim of a poor remake by a group of several inconsequential small-time pop divas in 2001.

LaBelle broke up just two years later, but Nona Hendryx enjoyed some success in the hard R&B field, and Patti LaBelle became a huge star in the mid-'80s, her hair huge as ever.

5. **THE SEX PISTOLS**

Many think the Sex Pistols were a glorious proletariat accident. Not so. Working-class some of them were, but designer Vivian Westwood and manager/entrepreneur Malcolm McLaren used their design savvy and marketing smarts to hoist the four protopunks to success.

Lead singer Johnny Rotten (né Lydon) and the rest of the band (drummer Paul Cook, guitarist Steve Jones, and bassist Glen Matlock, later replaced by Sid Vicious) were up to the task and certainly weren't puppets. The four played stripped-down, highly charged rock and were wild onstage and off. Their scruffy appearance and unkempt, unwashed hair, styled into elegantly dirty mops, changed British style overnight.

Punk quickly became a scene of styled anti-style, but the Pistols did it first (and best). Their mix of thrift-store sleaze and studied arrogance doesn't seem nearly as dated as the mass of leather, piercings, and torn jeans that followed.

6. THE B-52s

In Athens, Georgia, in the mid-'70s, there wasn't much for wild kids to do but dress up and dance. Five of them (Fred Schneider, Kate Pierson, Cindy Wilson, Ricky Wilson, and Keith Strickland) decided, as a joke, while sitting at a Chinese restaurant, to form a band and name it after slang for a bouffant hairdo.

It didn't matter that they weren't virtuosos. The Bs could lay down a beat, thanks to Strickland's drumming, and Pierson's keyboard skills and

Ricky Wilson's surf-via-Beefheart guitar lent enough to the equation to make them danceable.

Visually, they were spectacular. The guys had short haircuts and wore thrift-store vintage, while Kate and Cindy wore wild costume jewelry, splashy clothes, and bright makeup, and topped it off with the wildest collection of wigs any rock act has ever seen.

They quickly gained attention among New York hipsters and eventually signed a record deal with Warner Brothers in 1979. An unlikely band of stars they were, but the B-52s sold millions, appeared on *Saturday Night Live,* and became de rigeur fodder for party tapes for the next 20 years.

After four enjoyable albums, Ricky Wilson died of AIDS, but the Bs returned with style for 1989's *Cosmic Thing* album and hit singles "Love Shack" and "Roam." Although the ladies were older, their bouffants were intact.

7. THE STRAY CATS

The Stray Cats picked up their sound style from '50s rockabilly, country, and rock artists, the Beatles, and classic soul. But everything they did was over the top—especially their hair.

Brian Setzer, Lee Rocker, and Slim Jim Phantom were from Long Island, New York, but journeyed to England in the early '80s. Why?

Britain has a huge rockabilly cult, embracing music that Americans have forgotten that they created. The Stray Cats repaid their over-the-pond fans with "Rumble in Brighton," a song about the mid-'60s fights between rockers and mods at a British seaside resort town.

However, as much as the Stray Cats loved Britain, they were even happier to make it big back home in 1982 with "Rock This Town." Why? Only their hairdressers know for sure. As Setzer said at the time, "There's a hairspray called Final Net we used in New York. Can't get it here. English hairspray is trash."

8. BOY GEORGE

George O'Dowd, a London singer who was comfortable exploring his feminine side, hooked up with Culture Club in 1981.

Boy George, as he renamed himself, could sing everything from soul pastiches to show tunes. He, and the band, were perfect for the times, and as successful in the States as in their homeland. Singles like "Karma Chameleon," "Do You Really Want to Hurt Me?" and "Church of the Poison Mind" defined the catchy but inconsequential pop sound of the early '80s.

George was a lightning rod for controversy, with his girlish makeup; long, dreadlocked, styled, ribboned, and/or dyed hair; and unisex clothing. "Androgynous" was too weak a word for the cross-sexual identity he exuded. Even in later years, when he kicked drugs and cut his hair short, Boy George was comfortable crossing lines others wouldn't get near.

9. **TWISTED SISTER**

Five guys from Long Island dedicated to serious rocking out, Twisted Sister revitalized glam rock for the '80s with their wild makeup and outrageous hairdos following in the footsteps of Slade, Kiss, and T. Rex.

Lead singer Dee Snider (who was later called in front of a congressional panel to discuss "obscene" rock lyrics) had a frizzy blond 'do the *Designing Women* ladies would have been proud of. He and his mates played tough music for tough people, ignoring the question of whether tough guys actually wear hair gel and makeup.

The Sister's music was as bold and brash as their appearance. Their hit singles, "I Wanna Rock" and "We're Not Gonna Take It," as well as their videos, set them in opposition to (perceived) anti-rock people who wanted to deny the masses their right to bang their hairy heads.

10. SINÉAD O'CONNOR

Plenty of male rockers had featured shaved heads in the past, but a beautiful Irish woman?

Sinéad O'Connor was just 21 when her first album, the rock-oriented *Lion and the Cobra,* was a hit. Angry, passionate, and sometimes confused, O'Connor lashed out, often with good reason, against political enemies, former friends, and the record industry. When she shaved her head, she was targeted as androgynous, but she was simply expressing her femininity in her own way, which most (male) rock critics couldn't understand.

She would later do some acting, quit the music industry and rejoin it, regrow her hair and cut it off again, become an ordained priestess, proclaim her lesbianism, and get married. O'Connor also expanded her musical palette to include folk and torch standards before a return to rock with 2000's *Faith and Courage,* which included the outstanding "No Man's Woman."

Is It My name?

Sometimes it takes two, three, or more attempts to settle on a really good band name. (British ska/pop band Madness started out, for example, as the North London Invaders, then as Morris & the Minors. Not so great.) The following bands know all about the struggle to come up with a good, catchy, expressive name.

1. THE SUPREMES

When the Supremes first came together, they were neither Supreme nor a trio.

Diana Ross, Mary Wilson, Flo Ballard, and Barbara Martin began singing professionally in Detroit during the late '50s as the Primettes. The foursome did plenty of shows with the Primes (later the Temptations) and were known as the fellows' "sister group." Hence the name.

Eventually, Martin left, and the trio began to hang around Berry Gordy's Motown studio, begging for a chance to sing for the entrepreneur. It took until '60 for Gordy to sign the band, and he only did so on the condition they get a new name. Ballard chose "Supremes," which the other girls initially hated because of its perceived lack of femininity.

2. THE BEATLES

In their formative years, John Lennon and Paul McCartney were prone to nicknames, such as The Nerk Twins. When Lennon wrote an occasional humor column for *Mersey Beat* in the early '60s, he called himself "Beatcomber."

In the pre-Ringo days, the band called itself Johnny and the Moondogs. Lennon retitled himself "Johnny Silver," McCartney took the name "Paul Ramon," and George Harrison became "Carl Harrison," in honor of his idol, Carl Perkins.

Eventually, they went from Johnny and the Moondogs to Johnny Silver and the Silver Beatles, with "Beatles" chosen as a play on beat music and on Buddy Holly's Crickets. Finally, they shortened it to Beatles.

3. THE ROLLING STONES

In the early history of the World's Greatest Rock & Roll Band, whoever got the gig got the name, too.

Which was why, in 1962, the London-based R&B aggregation featuring Keith Richards, Brian Jones, and Ian Stewart, among others, was known as the Brian Jones Blues Band—Jones, the mover and shaker, was getting most of the gigs. He took extra payment for that, which caused some resentment, and occasionally called himself Elmo Lewis, assumedly to appear more authentically bluesy.

Then, after the band had acquired a lead singer, the group became Brian Jones and Mick Jagger and the Rollin' Stones. These were in the days before bassist Bill Wyman and drummer Charlie Watts. Once the classic five came together in early 1963, they settled on The Rolling Stones.

However, this didn't stop songwriters Jagger and Richards from using pseudonyms. They've referred to themselves as "Nanker Phelge" in many a songwriting credit and the "Glimmer Twins" as producers.

4. THE BYRDS

Folk singers Jim McGuinn, Gene Clark, and David Crosby came together after hearing the Beatles in early 1964. As an acoustic trio, they were known as the Jet Set.

Following the addition of drummer Mike Clarke and bassist Chris Hillman, they were relabeled The Beefeaters by a British Invasion-besotted Elektra Records for the 1964 "Please Let Me Love

You" single. That record failed, but the band continued to record, refining a style based on folk and folk-influenced songs, Beatlesque harmonies, and R&B rhythms.

The group hated being called The Beefeaters and eventually came up with The Byrds. Columbia used that new name for the early 1965 "Mr. Tambourine Man" single, and the rest is jangle-pop history.

5. STATUS QUO

Guitarist Fran Rossi, bassist Alan Lancaster, and drummer John Couglan, all from London, began playing in 1962 in various groups, including the Scorpions and the Spectres. Adding organist Roy Lynes, they recorded some unsuccessful singles, then took on guitarist Rick Parfitt in 1967.

Changing their name to Traffic (then to Traffic Jam when Steve Winwood's band hit it big), they continued to play whatever style of music was "in" at the time, be it Merseybeat, R&B, or psychedelia. Under the new name, Status Quo, they recorded the progressive hit singles, "Pictures of Matchstick Men" and "Ice in the Sun."

And they've stuck to the name Status Quo ever since. In 1970, they dropped Lynes, abandoned pop, and settled on three-chord, blues-based rock. This transition made them phenomenally successful. A British institution, the Quo remain together despite Lancaster's fractious departure in the '80s.

6. PINK FLOYD

The group that eventually would become Pink Floyd began at Regent Street Polytechnic Institute in London. Architecture students Rick Wright, Roger Waters, and Nick Mason, augmented by other musicians, were first called Sigma 6, then the T. Set, Meggadeth (Dave Mustaine, take note), the Abdabs, the Architectural Abdabs, and, finally, the Screaming Abdabs.

When guitarists Syd Barrett and Bob Close joined the core three in 1965 (Close left soon after), Barrett—who quickly became the leader of the group based on his singing, wild guitaring, and compositional ability—suggested an amalgam of two bluesmen's names, Pink Anderson and Floyd Council.

First known as The Pink Floyd Sound, the band later shortened their appellation to The Pink Floyd, and, by the early '70s, they were simply Pink Floyd, or "The Floyd" to their faithful.

7. CHICAGO

Meeting in February 1967 in a North Side Chicago apartment, the band that later made 26 albums (to date) formed as The Missing Links.

Next known as The Big Thing, the six-piece jazz-rock amalgam renamed themselves in 1968, this time to Chicago Transit Authority on the advice of producer James William Guercio, who had helped pioneer horn-driven pop with fellow Chicagoans The Buckinghams.

However, then-mayor Richard J. Daley threatened to sue over the name, the label for the city's bus and train system. As a result, the CTA simply became Chicago, though they had already moved to Los Angeles.

Later, the group would expand to seven with the 1968 addition of bass player and singer Peter Cetera, then eight when percussionist Laudir de Oliveira joined in 1974. The hits came fast and furious and continued well into the '90s.

8. SLADE

In 1966, Noddy Holder, Dave Hill, Jimmy Lea, and Don Powell formed the N'Betweens, playing the British rock of the day. Nothing special, they eventually changed their name to Ambrose Slade and embraced heavy rock (recording, oddly enough, the Beatles' "Martha, My Dear").

Chas Chandler, onetime bassist for the Animals and discoverer of Jimi Hendrix, who had embarked on a career in management, found them in London and remade Ambrose Slade as a "skinhead" band.

He had them dress in jeans, boots, and suspenders and cut off their hair.

When this failed, Chandler renamed them Slade and recast them as working-class boogie, advising them to use misspelled words in their song titles ("Mama, Weer All Crazee Now," "Cum on, Feel the Noize," "Gudbuy T'Jane").

This time, the formula was spot-on. Slade enjoyed an amazing 13 Top 5 British hits from 1971 to 1974, and their career continued into the '90s.

9. R.E.M.

April 5, 1980. Without a name just hours before their first gig (at a bombed-out former church that served as both their crash space and a community party haven), Athens, Georgia's, Bill Berry, Peter Buck, Mike Mills, and Michael Stipe asked friends to write suggestions in chalk on the church wall.

Some of the names submitted were Slut Bank, Cans of Piss, and Twisted Kites. None was seriously considered, but with no better alternative, they went with Twisted Kites until Stipe soon settled on the far more interesting and enigmatic R.E.M.

10. THE BANGLES

Four Southern California girls raised on the pop-rock of the '60s began playing in 1979. They originally called themselves The Colours, then The

Stuart Shea

R.E.M.'s Peter Buck, Mike Mills, and Bill Berry sign autographs in Chicago, July 1984.

Supersonic Bangs, then simply The Bangs. Sisters Debbie (drums) and Vicki (guitar) Peterson were augmented by guitarist Susannah Hoffs and bassist Annette Zilinskas.

They released the "Getting Out of Hand" 45 on their own Downkiddie label in 1981, but a New Jersey band soon laid legal claim to the name The Bangs.

After considering the situation, the ladies decided simply to change their name to "Bangles," a terrific move that emphasized both their sense of fun and their femininity. Soon, Zilinskas left the band, with Michael Steele (formerly of the Runaways) coming aboard. In 1984, the Bangles released their first album, *All Over the Place,* on Columbia.

You Can't Do That

B ack in the '60s, the wrong words could get you in trouble. The Byrds found their song about an airline voyage to England, "Eight Miles High," banned as a "drug song." In the '70s, standards were relaxed a bit, but even a band as big as Pink Floyd couldn't get the line, "Don't give me that do-goody-good bullshit" (from "Money") on AM radio. Nowadays, music and video contain such graphic images that much of the meaning is lost because of the need to chop out "objectionable content."

1. "RHAPSODY IN THE RAIN," LOU CHRISTIE

When Lou Christie's randy 1966 hit, "Lightnin' Strikes," climbed the charts all the way to #1, he quickly readied a follow-up. Sounding a lot like "Lightnin' Strikes," but with even sexier lyrics, the somewhat symphonic "Rhapsody in the Rain" spoke of "making out in the rain" and "making love in the storm."

At least it did until radio censors got a hold of it. As the record shot up the charts, some program directors and censors apparently decided that American decency was at stake. Christie was forced to rerecord his vocals and replace some of the "offending" words. "Rhapsody," altered enough so that its participants only "fell in love in the rain," stalled like a flooded engine. The record only made it to #16.

2. "OUTSIDE OF A SMALL CIRCLE OF FRIENDS," PHIL OCHS

Irony has never ruled the charts, and this record's sad tale proves it. In 1967, Ochs released this song in response to the 1964 Kitty Genovese tragedy, in which an entire New York neighborhood listened—but did nothing—as a young woman was murdered.

Ochs's composition, sung to a jangly piano-led backing track, bemoans a society in which people barricade themselves from others, lose their sense of humanity, and, ultimately, lose their freedoms.

The song's next-to-last verse raised plenty of hackles: "Smoking marijuana is more fun than drinking beer/But a friend of ours was captured and they gave him 30 years/Maybe we should raise our voices, ask somebody why/But demonstrations are a drag, and besides, we're much too high."

Clearly, this lyric indicted dope-smoking passivity, but smaller-minded radio program directors didn't see it that way. They forced A&M Records to edit the song. "A Small Circle of Friends," which had shown signs of breaking out on the singles chart, had to be pulled back and changed. As a result, it was stopped cold.

3. "BROWN-EYED GIRL," VAN MORRISON

Possibly the most popular song ever censored, Morrison's catchy R&B tale of sexual awakening was a subject of controversy when it first aired in 1967, but most stations played the song the way it was.

However, even today, many oldies radio stations have cut the "making love in the green grass" line and replaced it by repeating the words "slippin' and slidin'" from an earlier point in the song.

It's hard to understand why; far dirtier words are sung, and spoken, on the radio every day than "making love in the green grass."

4. "LET'S SPEND THE NIGHT TOGETHER," THE ROLLING STONES

The producers of CBS-TV's *Ed Sullivan Show* wanted the Stones to sing "Let's Spend the Night

Together," the flip side of their then-current hit, "Ruby Tuesday," in January 1967.

The Stones had been on the show the previous year, miming to "Paint It Black" and "Lady Jane" without incident, but Sullivan was uncomfortable with the new song's title and sentiment. (One wonders if he would have been equally uncomfortable with an "adult" entertainer, such as Jack Jones or Frank Sinatra, singing it.) Sullivan told the Stones to alter the song's title phrase to "Let's spend some time together" or they wouldn't be allowed to play.

After hours of arguing, the Stones went ahead and copped to this request, which now seems ridiculous. It's a tribute to their professionalism, and it's also hard to believe they really did it.

5. "KICK OUT THE JAMS," MC5

Detroit's White Panther-backed revolutionary space-rock protometal band, the Motor City Five (shortened to MC5) were into taking things all the way.

The *Kick out the Jams* album was recorded live at Detroit's Grande Ballroom in October 1968. The intro to the title track went, to great screams from the crowd, "And now...it's time...to... *Kick out the Jams, Motherfuckers!*"

One would assume that while Elektra Records, the MC5's label, professed belief in some sort of "revolution," it might not have wanted one quite like *that*. However, MC5 guitarist Wayne Kramer claims that Elektra executives wanted to release the album with the offending words included— spotlighted, in fact—to spark controversy.

Detroit's Hudson's department store refused to sell the album, so an alternate version, advising listeners to "Kick Out the Jams, brothers and sisters!" was released. It wasn't as compelling, but did get played on the radio.

A 45 release of "Kick Out the Jams" was a huge hit in Detroit and some other spots in the Midwest, but it was just the start of a rocky relationship between band and record company. The MC5 themselves took out an ad that read, "Fuck Hudson's," which certainly must have helped to smooth things out.

6. "BALLAD OF JOHN AND YOKO," THE BEATLES

With both George Harrison and Ringo Starr unavailable, John Lennon and Paul McCartney came together on April 14, 1969, to record John's new composition. "Ballad of John and Yoko" was an entertaining, if self-aggrandizing, tale of Lennon's life with new wife Yoko Ono.

As it was, many Beatles fans were unhappy not only with Lennon's relationship with Ono—a Japanese avant-garde artist seven years his senior—but also to the new single's chorus, which began with the line, "Christ! You know it ain't easy."

Some radio stations, fearing a religious backlash, didn't play the song at all. Some snipped the offending word out. Some cut the word, "Christ," and reinserted it into the song backward (!) to keep the flow of the song going. Any which way the record was played, "Ballad" was, not surprisingly, the least successful Beatles a-side since September 1964.

7. "JET AIRLINER," STEVE MILLER BAND

Miller, formerly a progressive blues musician in San Francisco in the late '60s, began to enjoy success as a singles artist in the '70s, finding his space-age blues/rock stew a good match for the times. "Jet Airliner," his fourth Top 10 single, made it up to #8 in May 1977.

On FM, the song was heard as written: "I don't want to get caught up in all that funky shit goin' down in the city." However, on Top 40 radio, Miller's "funky shit" was changed to "funky kicks"... whatever *they* were.

8. "MONEY FOR NOTHING," DIRE STRAITS

Dire Straits singer/songwriter/lead guitarist Knopfler took the sentiment for this song, and apparently some of the lyrics, from a conversation among furniture deliverymen. The blue-collar workers were railing against the cult of celebrity and the shallowness of rock music in the early '80s.

"That ain't working, that's the way you do it. You get a guitar on the MTV . . ." the lyrics went to "Money for Nothing."

At least those are the lyrics everybody heard. Not everybody heard the line, "That little faggot is a millionaire." Some stations refused to play that part for fear of offending more sensitive (or simply more easily offended) listeners.

9. "GIN AND JUICE," SNOOP DOGGY DOGG

Plenty of hip-hop and rap songs are edited for radio and MTV play. Pictures of marijuana leaves, athletic clothing logos, and guns are fuzzed out in videos; words are sliced from the middle of a line in many a rap, making the intent of some lyrics almost unintelligible unless you already know the song.

When, in early 1994, Snoop Dogg released this ode to the joys of hanging around with a drink and a smoke while cruising in his car, the line, "Smokin' indo, sippin' on gin and juice," was altered to "Smokin', smokin'." Apparently, MTV decided it was okay to play a video celebrating drinking while driving, but not one celebrating smoking weed.

10. "YOU DON'T KNOW HOW IT FEELS," TOM PETTY

"Let's get to the point," Petty sang in his 1994 release. "Let's roll another joint." Apparently believing that its viewers were either too naïve, too stupid, or too stoned to tell the difference, MTV chose to clip the word "joint" from the song, reverse it, and just stick it back onto the sound track of the song's video.

Didn't anyone consider the possibility that "Let's roll another tniooooooj" would have sounded even druggier than the original lyrics?

In the Street

For various reasons, certain cities have been centers of rock & roll: San Francisco, London, New York, L.A. (Let's forget about the ill-fated "Bosstown Sound" of the late '60s that caused Boston so much ridicule.)

But some homes of rock & roll are small college towns or unglamorous industrial cities that have contributed just as much as the average metropolis. John (Cougar) Mellencamp comes from Bloomington, Indiana; James Brown cut the epochal "Please, Please, Please" in Macon, Georgia. The Velvet Underground were not from Manhattan, but from Long Island. As the saying goes, it doesn't matter where you're from, it's where you're at.

1. TAMLA/MOTOWN

Berry Gordy worked on a production line at a Detroit car factory, but he dreamed of stamping out wax rather than auto parts. In 1958–59, he wrote "Lonely Teardrops" for Jackie Wilson and "You Got What It Takes" for Marv Johnson; both songs became big hits.

Gordy's brother-in-law, Harvey Fuqua, was a singer with the Moonglows and had his own record label. Gordy borrowed from his sister to finance his own label, which he called Tamla. His first release was Johnson's "Come to Me."

The company's first big hit was Barrett Strong's "Money," which rose to #23 on the pop charts (but was a much higher charter on the R&B scene) in early 1960. Strong would go on to write hit songs with Norman Whitfield for other Motown artists.

Next came the Miracles' "Shop Around," which shot all the way to #2 in late 1960 and early 1961. More super hits followed: the Marvelettes' "Please, Mr. Postman" was the label's first #1 in late 1961, and by 1964 Tamla/Motown was the foremost R&B imprint in the world and America's biggest independent record label.

This is not to say that all of the company's records were classics; Motown's production staff often bled a sound dry, making many of the label's biggest hits quite formulaic. However, the truly great records the label produced still endure.

Motown called itself "The Sound of Young America," which wasn't an exaggeration. The roster of the label's '60s acts includes some of the greatest performers in American music: The Temptations, Marvin Gaye, Stevie Wonder, The Supremes, Martha and the Vandellas, Smokey Robinson and the Miracles, The Four Tops, Mary Wells, The Jackson Five. Even the Isley Brothers, Gladys Knight, and the Four Seasons (!) spent some time in Gordy's stable.

Tamla/Motown and its sister labels, which included Soul, VIP, Gordy, Anna, MoWest, and Rare Earth, dominated the scene for many years. However, Motown lost some of its influence in the mid-'70s when disco came along; Gordy and his crew didn't care for the sound. In addition, smaller labels more in touch with local music scenes began to encroach on the R&B market.

2. LIVERPOOL

In the '50s, Liverpool, England, was one of that country's biggest seaports. Sailors brought all sorts of American goods—books, records, clothes—into the U.K. through the 'pool, making the industrial city on the Mersey River one of the land's secret enclaves of American culture.

While the rest of the world was bopping to the "teen idol" music of Fabian and Frankie Avalon in the early '60s, musicians from central and northern English towns like Liverpool, Manchester, and Birmingham played rock and R&B from the United States. Most of their songs were gleaned from obscure 45 RPM records transported through Liverpool.

It was only a matter of time before some of the more creative groups, like the Beatles, began writing their own material. Once the Beatles got a contract with Parlophone in 1962, and the "Liverpool Sound" began to break out, other bands from the north, such as Gerry and the Pacemakers, Billy J. Kramer and the Dakotas, Freddie and the Dreamers, and The Hollies, were signed and began to cut records.

The Liverpool Sound, also known as "Merseybeat," was full of chunky rhythm guitars, harmony vocals, quick tempos, and solid drumming. The Beatles, the Big Three, and the underrated Searchers were thought of at the time as Liverpool's top groups.

3. MEMPHIS

While the city has the same racial makeup as any other large southern city, Memphis music, at least, has always been a mix of black and white.

The two great record labels of the town have been fusions of country, gospel, and rhythm and blues: Sun Records, which did its great work in the '50s, and Stax, which helped define the sound of the '60s.

Sam Phillips, was born in Muscle Shoals, Alabama, in 1923. In 1950, after a few years as a disc jockey, he founded the Memphis Recording Service. His aim was to record "Genuine, untutored Negro music. Negroes with field mud on their boots and patches in their overalls...battered instruments and unfettered techniques."

In an era rife with racial prejudice, a white man taking on this task was bound to cause trouble. He made it worse by mixing his music; he not only recorded Roscoe Gordon, Rufus Thomas, and B.B. King, but also made inroads into country and western by recording the Johnny Burnette Trio.

Phillips truly loved western swing as well as black gospel and blues, and had a vision of putting them together. In 1952, he founded Sun Records to do it.

"If I could find a white man who had the Negro sound and Negro feel," he said, "I could make a billion dollars." Two years later, he found his man: Elvis Presley, who had come by the studio as early as 1953 hoping to be discovered, got a full-fledged audition with Phillips. The impresario teamed Presley with young guitarist Scotty Moore and bassist Bill Black, who were also playing a raw blues/country fusion.

Their first successful recording, 1954's "That's All Right," was the country/blues amalgam that Phillips was looking for; "rock & roll" had been born. Eighteen months later, Presley was on top of the world.

Phillips eventually sold Presley's contract to RCA, and used the money to record more white artists with the "rock & roll" bug, including Carl Perkins, Johnny Cash, Jerry Lee Lewis, Charlie Rich, and Roy Orbison.

Just a few years later, in 1959, country/western fiddle player Jim Stewart and local music fan Estelle Axton founded Satellite Records, soon renamed Stax as a play on the two principals' names. Axton's son, Charles, played sax with a local party band, the Mar-Keys, who would chart on Stax with the excellent instrumental "Last Night" in the summer of 1961.

Within two years, the company was Top 10 with Carla Thomas's "Gee Whiz." Carla's father, Rufus (who had worked with Sam Phillips) scored his own Top 10, "Walkin' the Dog," in November 1963.

The sound of Stax was pure Memphis soul: a mix of white and black styles played by white and black musicians. No other place in the music world had the racial harmony that existed in the Stax studio, and America lapped up the label's unmatchable sound.

The "house band" was Booker T. & the MGs, a racially mixed quartet that had its own hits, including the epochal "Green Onions." Guitarist Steve Cropper's clipped, understated melody lines offset the full, rich sound of organist Booker T. Jones. The rhythm section of bass guitarist Donald "Duck" Dunn and drummer Al Jackson set new standards for tightness and adventurous rhythms.

By 1967, Otis Redding and Sam and Dave (Stax artists produced in Memphis but released on the Atlantic label) were huge stars, and new acts like the Bar-Kays, Eddie Floyd, and Johnny Taylor, as well as established blues guitarist Albert King, were charting. "I Thank You," "Knock on Wood," "Hip-Hug-Her," "Tramp," "Born under a Bad Sign," and "Soul Man" were just some of the hits the label produced during 1966–68.

However, Sam and Dave's split and the airplane crash that claimed Redding and most of the Bar-Kays signaled an end to the first iteration of Stax.

Other artists, such as the Staple Singers, Isaac Hayes, the Emotions, and Little Johnny Taylor stepped into the breach. Booker T. & the MGs recorded their own music and continued to work on other artists' records. Stax remained a major force into the early '70s.

White groups remained represented on Stax as well; before-their-time popsters Big Star's 1972 and 1974 albums were on the label, although by that time the business side of Stax had deteriorated. By 1975, Stax was bankrupt.

4. NEW YORK

There has always been plenty of good rock music produced in the Big Apple. In the late '50s and early '60s, doo-wop-influenced white ethnic bands like Four Seasons and Dion and the Belmonts ruled the roost. By the mid-'60s, girl groups such as the Ronettes and pop-rockers like the Left Banke and the Cyrkle jousted for position with the more surreal, outré sounds of the Fugs and the Velvet Underground.

The mid-'70s saw New York undergo another cultural renaissance. Such bands as The New York Dolls, Talking Heads, Television, The Fast, Blondie, and the Ramones exploded out of Manhattan, providing America and England with music a million miles away from progressive rock, singer-songwriter fluff, and banal pop.

Ironically, the "new wave" bands of the time took elements from all the sounds of New York's great rock past: doo-wop and girl-group sounds, pop and psychedelic rock, experimental music, and classically influenced noise. Some bands, such as the B-52s and the dBs, eventually migrated to the Apple. Other locals, such as the Smithereens and Fleshtones, began careers that would span more than two decades.

In addition, by the early '80s, visual and literary artists such as William Burroughs, Laurie Anderson, and Lydia Lunch were combining their talents with music, often collaborating with seminal New York musical figures like Lou Reed, Tom Verlaine, and saxophonist John Zorn.

Current bands like Sonic Youth and Hall of Fame mine the city's rich heritage, combining their own visions with those of contemporary hip-hop, noise, and pop musicians. Their efforts keep New York's ever-shifting musical sands in the nation's sunlight.

5. PHILLY SOUL

Combining the fluid rhythms of the Motown and Stax sound of the '60s, but adding symphonic touches and Beatlesque production tricks, producers Kenny Gamble and Leon Huff and Thom Bell created a new style.

Gamble and Huff first worked their magic in the late '60s with the Delfonics, Archie Bell and the Drells, and Jerry Butler. Bell, who would later work with Elton John, had enjoyed success with Harold Melvin and the Blue Notes in the early '70s.

Bell leapt at the chance to produce the Spinners, who had left Motown in 1972. His first record with them, "I'll Be Around," was the initial salvo in a string of 11 Top 40 hits through 1980.

The O'Jays, who began as a five-piece in Ohio back in 1958, found success in the early '70s with a great series of Gamble/Huff songs, including "Back Stabbers," "Love Train," "I Love Music," and "For the Love of Money." They and the Three Degrees ("When Will I See You Again?") were mainstays of Gamble and Huff's Philadelphia International record company.

The PI label also produced one of the enduring dance hits of the era, "TSOP" ("The Sound of Philadelphia"), recorded by the label's house band, a multiracial group named MFSB, which stood for "Mothers, Fathers, Sisters, Brothers." First used as the theme of the *Soul Train* TV show, "TSOP" was a #1 smash in 1974.

Philly soul boasted a plethora of talent. Billy Paul ("Me and Mrs. Jones"), Teddy Pendergrass ("If You Don't Know Me by Now"), and Russell Tompkins, Jr., of the Stylistics (who scored ten Top 40 hits in two and a half years) are among soul's greatest vocalists. The sumptuous sound of

Gamble/Huff and Bell's productions complemented those honeyed voices perfectly.

Gamble, Huff, and Bell mingled modern production techniques with classic soul sounds to produce a sophisticated, affecting style of music echoed in every contemporary R&B ballad.

6. ATHENS, GEORGIA

Funny how boredom and drugs can wake up a little college town.

In the early '70s, bored by soft-rock and hippie jamming, glam-rock fans Keith Strickland, Kate Pierson, and Fred Schneider met at the University of Georgia. Soon the group of friends expanded, with siblings Ricky and Cindy Wilson hanging around.

A few years later, the five decided to form a band to play at local parties, and the B-52s were born. Their blend of thrift-store kitsch, funky art-dance rock, and good ol' southern charm made them the toast of the town. Parties, most of which featured plenty of sex, drugs, and rock & roll, were the style of Athens at the time, and that's where the Bs got their early exposure.

While other bands, such as the Fans and the Brains, had tried to play new music in Georgia, they didn't catch on like the Bs did. Other popular bands followed: Pylon, the Side Effects, the

Method Actors, Love Tractor, and, in February 1980, R.E.M.

Following the success of the B-52s, Pylon, and R.E.M., Athens became a hub of music-industry activity. Plenty of bands were signed whether they were good or not; a film *(Athens: Inside/Out)* was made; many parties were held.

Then, the inevitable anti-Athens backlash pushed the town back out of the spotlight. But experimental '60s-influenced bands such as Olivia Tremor Control and Neutral Milk Hotel continue to make records, and R.E.M.'s Michael Stipe still lives there.

7. THE SOUND OF YOUNG SCOTLAND

Punk rock hits Scotland! The smart-alecks involved in Glasgow's small but vital punk scene included entrepreneur Alan Horne, who founded Postcard Records with singer/guitarist Edwyn Collins. The Postcard logo was a cute but scruffy cat, and the label's slogan was the Motown-influenced joke, "Postcard: The Sound of Young Scotland."

What kind of music did the scruffy kitty play? The premier groups on the Postcard label were Orange Juice (which featured Collins), Aztec Camera, and Josef K.

All three bands were heavily influenced by current punk groups such as the Buzzcocks; by classic soul and R&B; and by '60s bands, including the

Velvet Underground, Syd Barrett's Pink Floyd, and—in Orange Juice's case, at least—Creedence Clearwater Revival.

The snappy, catchy sound found on most Postcard releases still influences indie pop groups today, although all the groups who recorded on the label have since capitulated.

8. MINNEAPOLIS

In the '80s, funk and punk both exploded all over the Twin Cities. Prince Rogers Nelson began to twirl his nasty brand of funk-rock with a loose cadre of backing musicians, while Morris Day and the Time followed. Prince filmed most of his *Under a Cherry Moon* film in his hometown.

In addition, several rock groups also made their mark in the Me Decade. Husker Du's supersonic punk attack shattered eardrums and cut a swath through the underground; the Replacements' disorganized charm and Paul Westerberg's perceptive songs got them a major label deal; Soul Asylum went through an early punk stage before hitting it big with "Runaway Train."

Not bad for a city whose biggest contributions to rock in the past had been the 1963 hit, "Surfin' Bird," and the 1979 disco novelty, "Funky Town."

Minneapolis never became the media center that Athens did, or Seattle would in the years following.

That's probably to the city's benefit; there are still plenty of good musicians in town.

9. MADCHESTER

The 1968 musical, *Hair,* hailed "Manchester, England, England" as the center of some sort of hip European cultural/rock mecca.

But back in the '60s, northern industrial center Manchester didn't boast much more than The Hollies, admittedly one of Britain's finest pop bands. By the early '80s, several bands borne from punk rock's "anyone can do it" ethos had kicked down the door. The Smiths, Joy Division (who evolved into New Order), and the world-famous Hacienda dance club and Factory Records label brought rock back north.

At the end of that decade, much of the industry was bankrupt, and the city's youth needed optimism. The rise of acid house music and a reinfusion of psychedelic drugs led to a rock-dance fusion labeled "Madchester," with bands like Stone Roses, Happy Mondays, The Charlatans, and Inspiral Carpets playing late-'60s-influenced rock with hyper dance beats and wearing "baggy" clothing.

While the movement faded out of style in just a few months amid violence and exploitation, other acts such as Urban Cookie Crew and Sub

Sub played on. New Order released a new CD just last year, and Manchester remains vital.

10. **SEATTLE**

The grunge movement, most popularly expressed by groups like Nirvana, Pearl Jam, Soundgarden, and Screaming Trees, took elements both from punk and '70s hard rock and brought a big dose of testosterone back to the music scene in the early '90s.

The sound really started, however, with earlier bands like Mudhoney, guitar wildmen whose "Touch Me, I'm Sick" was a protogrunge landmark, and the Melvins, who diverted from hardcore in that they played loud and rough, but molasses slow.

The rock scenes of Olympia and Seattle were havens for classic punk, stadium rock, beer, and, often, harder drugs. Nirvana, led by troubled manchild Kurt Cobain, recorded an LP, *Bleach,* that drew some major-label feeders. Once the group's 1991 *Nevermind* album was an unexpected hit, record companies snapped up all sorts of long-haired, facially fuzzed, guitar-toting lumberjack types.

While come-lately aggregations like Candlebox and Stone Temple Pilots mined the trend, the truly innovative bands—Nirvana, Pearl Jam, Soundgarden, and Hole (led by Courtney Love,

Cobain's wife and a future fashion model and actress), for instance—reinfused rock with a vitality that went beyond fashion, hairstyles, or videos.

Pearl Jam's Eddie Vedder proved to be a fine lyricist backed by a good, solid rock unit; Love screamed and cooed terrific songs as her band bashed away. Soundgarden's Kim Thayil established himself as a certified guitar hero, and the band's "Black Hole Sun" provided grunge with one of its classic singles.

The grunge movement, as it was, died out, as all media-driven rock trends seem to—in a haze of lousy wannabe bands, heroin, and overexposure. Cobain's death in 1994 rang the curtain down on grunge as a musical force, with Nirvana drummer Dave Grohl courting MTV with the Foo Fighters and the region's other bands working to distance themselves from the city's heritage. New York's Smithereens put a headstone on grunge with "Sick of Seattle."

Gotta Serve Somebody

When George Harrison began playing the sitar and chanting mantras in the '60s, he brought spirituality into the rock & roll forefront for the first time. But the late Beatle wasn't the first, or last, rock singer to feel a higher calling.

1. LITTLE RICHARD

Coming from a gospel background (he was raised as a Seventh-Day Adventist), "Little" Richard Penniman always struggled with his career as a rock & roll belter and with his life as a gay man living in a straight time.

During a 1957 tour of Australia, the pressure became too much. After a close call on an airplane, Penniman tossed his jewelry off a bridge, broke down, and declared himself lost and in need of salvation. Little Richard retired and reembraced Jesus.

Months of intense religious study followed. "If God can save me, an old homosexual, he can save anybody," Richard Penniman would say years later. He signed with Gone Records in 1959 as a gospel artist.

He didn't record secular music again until 1963, when he felt he could reconcile his love for music (and his need to make a living) with his beliefs. Little Richard rerecorded his old hits more than once, and when '50s rock came back in vogue in the late '60s, he was ready.

Although he has (again) veered from rock music to Jesus and back in the last 30 years, Penniman remains a popular concert singer and talk show guest.

2. PETER GREEN/JEREMY SPENCER

Fleetwood Mac's original guitarists, Peter Green and Jeremy Spencer, brought different disciplines to the band. Green had played with John Mayall's Bluesbreakers; Spencer excelled at imitations of early rockers, such as Buddy Holly.

However, both of them wound up leaving Fleetwood Mac once the group became stars. After "Albatross," "Man of the World," and "Oh, Well" all reached the top of the British charts, Green—the group's foremost composer—departed the Mac in 1970, leaving rock music in favor of spiritual contemplation. The desperation and misery he sang about in "Oh, Well" was clearly autobiographical.

Green reemerged playing blues in the late '90s, looking somewhat the worse for the wear.

Just a year later, Spencer, who had taken over much of the workload after Green's departure, made a split-second decision to join the Children of God religious organization while the band was in Los Angeles. He never returned to rock, and it took the Mac until 1976 to get back on the charts.

3. CARLOS DEVADIP SANTANA

The phenomenal rise of Santana to the forefront of American bands in the early '70s took its toll on all the group's members. Everyone involved was struggling with a different type of drug, and, by 1972, much of the community spirit of the aggregation had evaporated. Carlos Santana, feeling the pressure of having to keep an increasingly large and both musically and interpersonally complex troupe together, was searching for help.

His British friend, John McLaughlin, a guitarist who had played with Brian Auger, Miles Davis, and Buddy Miles, had become a convert of Bengalese mystic Sri Chinmoy and eventually founded the Mahavishnu Orchestra. Santana liked what he heard and began studying Sri Chinmoy as well.

Eventually Santana became a convert and adopted the name Devadip, after which he and McLaughlin recorded the *Love Devotion Surrender* album in 1974. Santana disbanded the original group and its excesses, got his personal habits under control, and eventually made several comebacks, including a Grammy-winning album, *Supernatural,* in 1999.

4. DAN PEEK

America (Dan Peek, Dewey Bunnell, and Gerry Beckley) were one the top groups of the mid-'70s, working as a sort of poor man's Crosby, Stills, and Nash. Critics didn't love them, but America collected seven Top 20 singles on the U.S. charts in three years.

However, ten years of playing and traveling together had begun to wear on the participants. Seeking something greater in his life, and wanting to find joy rather than envy and disgust in music, Peek had a spiritual awakening and left America in 1976. His first solo LP, a Christian affair, *All Things Are Possible,* spawned a hit single in the title track and garnered two Grammy nominations.

The other two members of America had hits into the '80s, while Peek continues to record and tour as a solo artist.

5. **B.J. THOMAS**

In just three years, Thomas went from obscure Oklahoma country/soul singer to crooner of MOR movie themes. And the weirdness was just starting.

In 1966, Thomas had a hit with a Tex-Mex version of Hank Williams's "I'm So Lonesome I Could Cry." He then notched pop-soul chart entries with "Eyes of a New York Woman" and "Hooked on a Feeling" before his biggest hit, the 1969 #1 "Raindrops Keep Falling on My Head," Burt Bacharach and Hal David's theme from the smash film *Butch Cassidy and the Sundance Kid.*

Unfortunately, by the time of his second #1, 1974's "(Hey, Won't You Play) Another Somebody Done Somebody Wrong Song?" Thomas was addicted to cocaine and amphetamines. Two years later, Thomas's estranged wife introduced him to two friends who helped him to pray. On January 26, 1976, Thomas gave his life to Christ.

In 1981, Thomas—who had rebuilt his career as an inspirational and country artist—joined the Grand Ole Opry. He still tours and records, playing both his old hits and newer music.

6. **GLEN CAMPBELL**

Campbell, an expressive singer and guitar virtuoso, has played with acts as diverse as the Beach

Boys, The Monkees, and The Champs (who recorded "Tequila") and has sung hit songs written by Allen Toussaint, John Hartford, and Jimmy Webb.

"By the Time I Get to Phoenix" (1967) was the first of his 21 Top 40 hits, which included two #1 smashes: "Rhinestone Cowboy," from 1975, and 1977's "Southern Nights." Perhaps his most beautiful recording was Webb's "Wichita Lineman," an aching story of a lonely guy that rose to #3 in 1969.

But by the '80s, with the hits a memory, Campbell was drinking too much and taking too many pills. While he continued to tour, Campbell felt lost until he rediscovered his spiritual roots.

Campbell's long-dormant Christianity reawakened and led to a decision to record three spiritual albums in the '90s. Earlier marriages ended in heartbreak, and relationships with his older children remain strained, but Campbell—in a new marriage with new children and a new outlook—appears to be together.

7. BOB DYLAN

Dylan had long used religious imagery in his songs, both for comic and serious purposes. However, following 1978's *Street Legal* album, Dylan experienced a Christian epiphany.

He recorded three albums, *Slow Train Coming,*
Saved, and *Shot of Love,* consisting almost entirely
of spiritually based material. He put his songs in
the hands of a solid R&B backing band and, at
times, shared the mike with vocalist Clydie King.

Some of his best-loved songs, such as "Every
Grain of Sand" and "Gotta Serve Somebody," come
from this period, as does some of his least appealing moralizing. (John Lennon, possibly still smarting
from Dylan's 1966 song, "4th Time Around," a
parody of "Norwegian Wood," recorded an unreleased jab at Dylan, "Serve Yourself.")

In the early '80s, Bobby D. (who had also
messed around with Judaic imagery earlier in his
career) refined his vision into a more straightfor-
ward package, releasing more lyrically straight-
forward rock material.

8. MARK FARNER

Grand Funk Railroad's fuzzed-out, crushing
thump was called, "The all-time loud white noise"
by Rod Stewart in the '70s. Fans loved the
Michigan trio, whose name was a pun on Grand
Trunk Railroad; the press couldn't stand them.

Guitarist Mark Farner, bassist Mel Schacher,
and drummer Don Brewer were a smash, with hit
albums produced by Todd Rundgren and Frank

Zappa and top-selling singles like "We're an American Band," "The Loco-Motion," and "Bad Time." But by 1977, Grand Funk had imploded.

In 1983, Farner's wife left him, and he began drinking heavily. In search of a solution, Farner remembered praying when he was nine years old, after the death of his father, and experienced a spiritual awakening.

Anything but a choirboy during his Grand Funk days, Farner asked for forgiveness. He dedicated himself to Jesus, and his wife returned. But he didn't stop rocking; while Farner spent the late '80s and early '90s playing with a band called the God Rockers (soft-pedaling was never Farner's strong suit), he also put in stints as part of Ringo Starr's All-Star Band and several reunited versions of Grand Funk.

9. CAT STEVENS (YUSEF ISLAM)

The R&B singer-turned-balladeer racked up million-selling singles and albums throughout the '70s, but always sounded like someone who hadn't quite decided what or where he wanted to be.

After moving to Brazil in the mid-'70s to escape the punitive British tax system, Stevens became involved in charities and developed his spiritual interests further. After forays into different paths, he became a Muslim in 1979 and changed his name to Yusef Islam.

While he served as a peacemaker between the British and Saddam Hussein during the Gulf War, Islam made enemies for his support of the *fatwa* (an order to kill in the name of Allah) against "blaspheming" author Salman Rushdie, author of *The Satanic Verses.*

Islam claims that his statements were misunderstood. However, 10,000 Maniacs chose to remove a version of his 1972 hit, "Peace Train," from later pressings of their popular *In My Tribe* album.

Following the September 11, 2001, tragedies in New York and at the Pentagon, outside Washington, D.C., Yusef Islam uncategorically stated his horror and shock at the attacks.

10. **AL GREEN**

Born into a gospel-singing family, Green had his first hit in 1967 but did not become a star until 1970, after he had started working with producer Willie Mitchell at Hi Records in Memphis. Green's smoldering, sweet soul music sounded different from anything else, and he became a huge star.

An idol for both his expressive voice and his smooth, sexy approach, Green sang his love songs with a burning, religious fervor, and his fans adored

him. Unfortunately, such adulation had its disad-
vantages.

The much-retold 1974 "Grits Incident," in
which a woman infatuated with Green reacted to
his spurning her by pouring hot cereal on him and
severely burning him, was a major factor in his
decision to reembrace his spirituality. In 1976,
Green was ordained as a minister and began
preaching as well as recording both gospel and
secular music.

Play Misty for Me

I n dance clubs and on the radio, the disc jockey has always been a mythic figure, be it the old-time entertainer at a '50s sock hop, the '60s "in-crowd" radio record spinner, or the superstar disco, house, or techno turntablist of today. And there have been plenty of songs extolling, pleading with, and criticizing them.

1. "BRISTOL STOMP," THE DOVELLS

In this 1961 Top 5 hit, about a dance craze sweeping a small town in the Philadelphia suburbs, the Dovells paid tribute to "The kids in Bristol [who] are sharp as a pistol when they do the Bristol Stomp."

That's the kind of fun but lightweight stuff that passed for rock music back in the pre-Beatle era, when teen idols, shiny-smiled 14-year-old girls, and the occasional surfer or soul singer made the music played on the radio.

It certainly didn't hurt the Dovells' chances to get their record played when they inserted a little tribute to the record-spinners who worked at teen dances: "It started in Bristol at a DJ hop; they hollered and whistled, never wanted to stop. We ponied and twisted, and we rocked with Daddy G."

The Dovells racked up four Top 40 hits, including "Bristol Twistin' Annie," peaking with 1963's manic dance number "You Can't Sit Down." Len Barry, the Dovells' lead singer, left the group after "You Can't Sit Down" and would enjoy a huge solo hit in 1965 with "1-2-3."

2. "LEGEND OF PAUL REVERE," PAUL REVERE & THE RAIDERS

This story song, which told in humorous terms the tale of the popular military-garbed rock band that rode in from the Northwest, was the b-side of the group's 1967 hit single, "Him or Me: What's It Gonna Be?"

The chorus of the song implored disc jockeys not to forget about the band: "All you stations, across the nation, please play our records for your congregation."

Of course, forgetting about the Raiders was not really an option. From 1966 to 1971, they were one of the country's most popular teen acts, placing 11 hits in the Top 20. Most of their biggest hits accompanied the exposure garnered from being featured performers on TV's *Where the Action Is* and *Happening* programs.

3. "MURRAY THE WHY," THE CYRKLE

This song only saw the light of day on the soundtrack to the 1969 film, *The Minx,* and has never been reissued on any Cyrkle compilation.

And it's not hard to understand the reason. This song, featuring lyrics clearly addressed to ever-so-hip '60s New York DJ Murray "The K" Kaufman, is more than a little barbed.

"Who cops an attitude? Murray the why. Why, why, why why, why??" sang the Cyrkle, themselves a New York group (who were managed, incidentally, by Brian Epstein and his associate, Nat Weiss. John Lennon named the Cyrkle).

The four songs on the film's soundtrack were the last songs to be credited to the Cyrkle, whose big hits, "Red Rubber Ball" and "Turn-Down Day," had been released back in 1966. The Cyrkle's Don Danneman and Tom Dawes would later write advertising jingles, including the popular "Plop-Plop-Fizz-Fizz" antacid song of the '70s.

4. "WOLFMAN JACK," TODD RUNDGREN

Todd Rundgren's 1972 double-album *Something/Anything* contains several of his best-loved songs. "I Saw the Light," "Hello, It's Me," "It Wouldn't Have Made Any Difference," and "Couldn't I Just Tell You" make *S/A* one of the most influential pop albums ever.

Also included was this hard rock/soul number, a salute to the legendary DJ from rock's early days. "Hey, baby! You're the subliminable [sic] trip to nowhere! You'd better get your trip together before you come in here with us," he yelps in tribute to the Wolfman's nutty dialogue.

"You better come back to Wolfman Jack," Rundgren wails, fortifying himself with several over-dubbed voices (his own) meant to simulate those of classic female background singers.

But despite a spoken-word bridge in which Rundgren seems to imitate the classic DJ, he's as much singing about a wolflike sex machine out to seduce his woman as he is about a record-spinner. "When the moon shines bright and everything's all right, the Wolfman creeps into town. . . . If I catch you after dark walkin' in the park, I'm liable to do something bad!"

5. "CLAP FOR THE WOLFMAN," THE GUESS WHO

"Da Doo Ron Ron and the Duke of Earl they were friends of mine," the Guess Who's lead singer, Burton Cummings, sings to begin this catchy but somewhat bizarre 1975 Top 10 hit.

Over a combination of tremoloed guitars and reggae-based piano, Burton tells us how much he digs the rock & roll music on his car radio. The problem is, the girl he's romancing likes the music even more, and when he tries to get close to her in the back seat, she's more interested in listening to "the cat on the radio"—Wolfman Jack.

The Wolfman himself makes several cameos on the record, at one point joyfully deflating Cummings's fading hopes: "You thought she was diggin' *you*, but she was diggin' *me!*"

6. "DJ," DAVID BOWIE

Much of David Bowie's work involves exposing the banality and desperation of characters who appear invincible. The club DJ is one of the poor saps who has felt the sting of the Bowie knife.

Lodger (released in 1979 and featuring the smash, "Boys Keep Swinging") includes "DJ," a swinging tune with some less-than-complimentary lyrics.

"I've got a girl out there, I suppose . . . I think she's dancing. What do *I* know? I am a DJ, I am what I play. Can't turn around. I am a DJ, I am what I play . . . I got believers, kiss-kiss. I got believers."

It was a Top 30 single in the U.K., but got no higher. Those blasted DJs.

7. "PILOT OF THE AIRWAVES," CHARLIE DORE

This plaintive, country-flavored tune was a major worldwide hit in early 1980, reaching #13 on the American charts.

Ms. Dore's sweet, tuneful delivery of this melancholy song about a lady in love with a disc jockey was similar in style and arrangement to some of Olivia Newton-John's country songs of the early '70s.

"Play the record of your choice. I don't mind; I'd be happy just to hear your voice," she sang about her favorite DJ. "You make the nighttime race . . . I don't need to see your face. You're sounding good to me."

Discovered in London by Chris Blackwell, president of Island Records, Dore recorded "Pilot of the Airwaves" on her very first album. While she didn't enjoy any more chart hits in America, Charlie Dore remains an international singing star and songwriter and has acted in several popular films and stage shows in her native England.

8. "PANIC," THE SMITHS

In this 1986 single about mob mentality, based (musically) on T. Rex's "Metal Guru," the disconnection of ordinary young people from the things that should make them happy leads to violence.

"Burn down the disco . . . hang the blessed DJ," Morrissey sings over a glam-rock beat and shimmering guitars. "Because the music that they constantly play says nothing to me about my life."

As is the case with many of Morrissey's lyrics, it's hard to know just how serious he is. Nobody would argue that disliking a song is reason to kill someone, but the truth of England's cultural elite leaving common people in the cold is hard to deny.

Inspiring the lyric was Morrissey and guitarist Johnny Marr's disgust with BBC Radio's decision to play Wham's candy-floss single, "I'm Your Man," immediately following a news report on the Chernobyl nuclear tragedy.

This odd and fascinating song fades with a choir of schoolchildren singing, with gusto, "Hang the DJ, Hang the DJ, Hang the DJ . . ."

9. "RADIO SONG," R.E.M.

The leadoff track on the Georgia band's seventh album, *Out of Time,* began as a quiet number, with Michael Stipe singing about "the world collapsing around my ears," then changes into a rockin' diatribe about the stupid music playing on the radio.

This song was risky for R.E.M., and it hasn't aged well. Their first entry into soul-style music, "Radio Song" featured metallic guitar work, popping bass guitar, and southern-fried organ work, but still came across as somewhat ham-fisted.

"It's that same sad song. DJ sucks. Makes me sad," Stipe sings/speaks in a world-weary tone. At other times, Stipe's vocal is unusually histrionic, as is the rap by KRS-One (Kris Parker) at the song's fadeout. The rap puts the blame for . . . for . . . well, for *something bad* squarely on DJs.

"What are you sayin'? What are you playin'? . . . DJs communicating to the masses. Sex and violence classes," KRS raps. "Now our children grow up prisoners, all their life radio listeners!"

10. "MUSIC," MADONNA

A much more positive entreaty to DJs was the leadoff track of Madonna's 2000 *Music* CD. "Hey, Mr. DJ, put a record on. I want to dance with my baby," the chameleon-like superstar sang sassily. "I like to boogie woogie."

The song's backing track sounded as if Madonna had been listening to Middle Eastern music, Beck, and some old-school garage. Assisted by able producer Mirwais Ahmadzai, Madonna did it again—staying on top of the current dance scene and expanding her music to include new sounds. "Music" became a huge hit single and paved the way for the successful album that followed.

I Died Today

Singing and playing are dangerous jobs. Besides the obvious threats like drugs, infidelity, and alcohol, there is the constant strain on the voice and body; the threats of jealous, angry, or crazy "fans"; and the endless lines of electrical cable. Not everyone gets out of rock music—or even a routine concert—alive. The performers on this list perished rehearsing or onstage or passed away later from injuries received while onstage.

1. TAMMI TERRELL

Honey-voiced Tammi Montgomery released her first record in 1961, when she was just 15. By 1967, she was dating Temptations singer David Ruffin and recording for Motown with Marvin Gaye.

Marvin and Terri became one of soul music's great duets, scoring five Top 20 hits in just 14 months, including classics like "Ain't Nothing Like the Real Thing" and "You're All I Need to Get By." The pair's amazing togetherness on record led to rumors of romance, but they were just wonderful collaborators.

The still-young Tammi did this despite a brain tumor. In late 1967, thinking she was simply suffering from stress-related migraines, the hard-working Terrell collapsed in Gaye's arms while performing at Hampden-Sydney College in Virginia.

She recovered enough to record again the next year, but never could shake her illness. After eight operations, the effects of which left her weighing just over 90 pounds, partially paralyzed, and unable to sing, Terrell died on March 16, 1970.

2. LINDA JONES

One of the first truly acrobatic soul singers, Linda Jones would influence "all-over-the-place" vocalists such as Chaka Khan, Mariah Carey, and Whitney Houston.

She first recorded in 1963, but didn't hit it big until July 1967, when her "Hypnotized" reached #21 for the tiny Loma label. Although Jones later recorded for several other labels, she never again had a hit but was well known for her live performances. She could rattle the windows with her unusual (grating, to some) vocal timbre.

Vitality of voice aside, her career would be brief. On March 14, 1972, at age 28, Jones fell into a diabetic coma while performing at Harlem's famed Apollo Theatre. She died shortly thereafter.

3. **LES HARVEY**

Bursting onto the U.K. rock scene in 1970, Scotland's Stone the Crows soon built a strong following. Singer Maggie Bell was seen by many as a British Janis Joplin, while guitarist Les Harvey (younger brother of raucous singer Alex Harvey) was much admired for his ability to play both hard rock and soul licks.

However, on May 3, 1972, Harvey was electrocuted on stage at Swansea, Wales's, Top Rank club when he accidentally touched an ungrounded microphone. Dazed and saddened, the band attempted to carry on with guitarist Jimmy McCulloch (who would later join Wings before dying of alcohol-related illness), but after one more album, the band threw in the towel.

4. **JOHN ROSTILL**

When popular English instrumentalists the Shadows lost bass player "Licorice" Locking to the Jehovah's Witnesses in 1963, they recruited John Rostill. The new guy came aboard just as the Shadows began to fall from favor with the rise of harder-edged British Invasion rockers. In 1968, the Shadows disbanded, even though they made sporadic comebacks over the next few years.

Rostill found an even bigger gig when he hooked up with hip-shaking Welsh song-belter Tom Jones in 1970. He remained with Jones until 1973, playing on live LPs and even passing up a Shadows reunion to continue touring. Unfortunately, on November 26, 1973, Rostill was electrocuted while working in his home recording studio. His wife and his fellow Shadows bandmate, Bruce Welch, found him.

5. **KEITH RELF**

The charismatic and popular singer for the Yardbirds had a British beat haircut, a Chicagoan's harmonica style, a Delta bluesman's drawl, and an ear for experimentation that captured influences as diverse as Gregorian chant, British folk, and Asian melodies.

After he left the foundering band in 1967, Relf and former Yardbirds drummer Jim McCarty played in two folk-influenced bands, Together and Renaissance. However, Relf never seemed to harness his ability, and he simply drifted from one musical situation to the next.

"Howlin'" Relf's story came to an end on February 14, 1976, when he died of electric shock.

He was playing an ungrounded guitar while standing near an open gas line in his basement studio.

6. **JACKIE WILSON**

Former amateur boxer Jackie Wilson was one of R&B's most exciting performers. He spent four years with The Dominoes, then went solo. His first big hits were "Reet Petite" and "Lonely Teardrops" in the late '50s; as good as his records were, they couldn't capture Wilson's in-concert magic.

In the '60s, he turned to soul, pumping out classics like "Baby Workout" and the classic "(Your Love Keeps Lifting Me) Higher and Higher." Although the hits dropped off in the early '70s, Wilson maintained a heavy touring schedule, bringing his excitement to the cabaret circuit.

He suffered a stroke on September 29, 1975, while performing at the Latin Casino in Cherry Hill, New Jersey. Wilson collapsed into a brain damage-induced coma, where he remained until finally passing away on January 21, 1984.

7. **"COUNTRY DICK" MONTANA**

Born Daniel McLain, six-foot, four-inch "Country Dick" was the much-loved singer and drummer for the '80s southern California roots rock/country foursome, The Beat Farmers. He also worked with other musicians of a similar stripe in the early '90s, including Mojo Nixon, Rosie Flores, and Dave Alvin.

Always a hard-partying, fast-living guy, Montana, nicknamed "The Last of the Grown Men," left the planet on November 8, 1995, at age 40, after suffering a massive heart attack while behind the drums on stage in British Columbia. He died, by the way, with his cowboy boots on.

8. JOHNNY "GUITAR" WATSON

The longtime bluesman wasn't just a garden-variety twelve-bar Delta guy. His mid-'50s instrumental, "Space Guitar," featured speedy playing and outrageous effects that Jimi Hendrix wouldn't discover for another decade.

By the '70s, his signature blues licks were no longer in vogue, so the forward-thinking guitarist moved into heavy funk, cutting R&B smashes like "Superman Lover" and "Real Mother for You."

Watson's CV also included recordings with '60s psychedelic band Kaleidoscope (in tandem with '50s singer Larry Williams) and singing Frank Zappa's bizarre "In France."

He remained popular both at home and abroad, but on May 17, 1996, Watson died at age 61 while playing at the Yokohama Blues Café in Yokohama, Japan.

9. MARK SANDMAN

Not many guitarless rock bands have made their mark, and even fewer had a lineup of bass, drums, and saxophone. Morphine was one.

Coming out of punk, soul, rock, and blues backgrounds, the members of Boston-based Morphine (Mark Sandman, once of Treat Her Right, on bass; Billy Conway on drums; and Dana Colley playing sax) recorded five albums. Sandman's specially developed two- and three-string bass guitars played a major part in creating the band's distinctive sound.

On July 3, 1999, Sandman was playing with Morphine at a show near Rome, Italy, when he suffered a fatal heart attack during "Mona's Sister," the second song of the band's set. He died before reaching a hospital. The 46-year-old Sandman had apparently been stabbed in the chest in the late '70s while driving a cab, which might help to explain why his heart gave out.

10. CURTIS MAYFIELD

Chicago's Curtis Mayfield was one of soul music's great innovators. His ability and willingness to use Latin rhythms, string arrangements, interesting vocal parts, and aggressive drumming on his records helped his trio, the Impressions, sound like nobody else. They scored ten Top 40 hits between 1958 and 1968.

During the next decade, Mayfield moved into funkier territory. His greatest achievement may have been the soundtrack for the 1972 antismack film, *Super Fly,* which included the title song and another smash, "Freddie's Dead." Mayfield was an outstanding producer as well as a great artist, crafting music for Jerry Butler (his old Impressions bandmate) and the Staple Singers. He remained vital into the '90s, recording with Ice-T and keeping his Curtom record label in business.

Mayfield was on stage preparing for a concert in New York City on August 13, 1990, when a bank of stage lights fell on him, leaving him paralyzed. He recovered only partially, losing his ability to play instruments and having trouble singing. Mayfield died, disconsolate, on December 26, 1999.

Cross Wires

S ome of these singer/actors promoted their records on their own TV shows. Some sang songs stapled to the soundtracks of popular films. All of them had hits, and most of them are far better known and respected for their acting. In general, an actor who records ten albums is going to be a far better and more imaginative musician than one who cuts one or two quick cash-ins.

1. RICKY NELSON

The original TV rock star, Ricky Nelson (1940–1985) was born into show business. His dad, Ozzie, was a bandleader and his mother, Harriet, a singer.

The four Nelsons (including Ricky's brother, David) were all featured on the TV situation comedy, *Ozzie and Harriet,* which ran from 1952 to 1966. America literally watched Ricky and David grow up, and this built-in publicity was critical when Ricky launched his singing career in 1957. "A Teenager's Romance," which reached #2 on the charts, was the first of 17 Top 10 hits he racked up through 1964.

He shortened his name to Rick in 1961 when he turned 21. While the hits slowed down, Nelson continued to make music. Blown off course by the winds of musical change, he disappeared from the charts in 1965, but returned in 1970 as a country artist with a version of Bob Dylan's "She Belongs to Me."

Two years later, Nelson hit the Top 10 for the last time with the catchy "Garden Party," an auto-biographical tale of playing an oldies show at Madison Square Garden.

2. WINK MARTINDALE

In 1950, 17-year-old Winston Martindale, of Jackson, Tennessee, began his career as a disc jockey. It would be a 50-years-and-counting profession.

He took a prime job as a DJ in Los Angeles, and, in 1959, was asked to record a 1948 country song, "Deck of Cards," a narrative about how a lonely soldier uses playing cards to remind him of things meaningful to him—God, family, and country.

This was Martindale's only Top 40 hit. He returned to disc jockey work, and then moved into television with *Teenage Dance Party.* In the '70s, he became famous for his work on game shows, including *Gambit* and *Tic Tac Dough.* He returned to TV in 1999 with *Debt* and still hosts a syndicated radio show, *The Music of Your Life.*

3. HAYLEY MILLS

The sprightly British actress became a star in her early teens, appearing in films like *Pollyanna* and *In Search of the Castaways.*

Mills's 1961 vehicle, *The Parent Trap,* in which she played identical twin sisters reunited at summer camp, featured a cute piece of teen fluff, entitled "Let's Get Together," that busted into the Top 10. The fact that Hayley Mills could barely carry a tune, even with a suitcase, was hardly relevant.

After the success of "Let's Get Together," her follow-up single, "Johnny Jingo," made #21 in April 1962, but that was it for Hayley Mills and music—until 1996, when her son, Crispian, rose to prominence as the lead singer and guitarist of the British psychedelic band, Kula Shaker.

4. PATTY DUKE

At 15, Patty Duke was a sensation as Helen Keller in the 1962 film version of *The Miracle Worker.* The next year, she moved over to television as the star of *The Patty Duke Show,* in which she played identical cousins (uh, yes, identical *cousins*), one from Britain, the other from Brooklyn Heights, New York.

Most young stars of the era ended up making records to try and broaden their appeal, whether they could sing or not. Duke's big hit was 1965's "Don't Just Stand There," a melodramatic, string-heavy, echo-laden waltz based on similar teen operettas sung by Leslie Gore, which made it to #8. A follow-up, "Say Something Funny," stalled at #22, and that spelled the end of Ms. Duke as a recording star.

5. THE AVANT GUARD (WITH CHUCK WOOLERY)

Raised in Ashland, Kentucky, Chuck Woolery bombed out of college, the Navy, and various jobs before teaming up with friend Bubba Fowler in Nashville and recording "Naturally Stoned" in 1968.

That was the only hit the short-lived group ever had, and it didn't get higher than #40 on the charts. But that bit of success whetted Woolery's appetite for show business, and he soon ended up doing movies and kids' TV shows (remember *The New Zoo Revue?*) before broadcasting mogul Merv Griffin advised him to get into game shows.

Woolery was the initial host of *Wheel of Fortune* in 1975 and has never looked back, except with humor.

6. VICKI LAWRENCE

Vicki got her big break in showbiz because of her physical resemblance to Carol Burnett. The two met at a beauty pageant in 1967, which Burnett judged (Lawrence won), and, before long, the two worked on Burnett's popular CBS-TV comedy/variety series.

In 1969, Lawrence married Bobby Russell, a songwriter responsible for the adult-contemporary, middle-of-the-road (MOR) standards, "Honey" and "Little Green Apples." Well-known producer Snuff Garrett tinkered with and recorded "The Night the Lights Went Out in Georgia," with Lawrence, heretofore an actress, singing.

Although the downbeat but catchy song went all the way to #1 in April 1973, Lawrence knew music wasn't to be her career. Her relationship with Russell was on the down escalator, and the pressure of recording an album to capitalize on the single's success while her marriage was coming apart was almost too much to bear. She later told *Billboard* magazine, "I kind of got out of music after that."

7. JOHN TRAVOLTA

Although he was already too old to be in high school when *Welcome Back, Kotter* first aired on

ABC, John Travolta was successful as Vinnie Barbarino on the sitcom from 1975 to 1977.

His popularity—based on acting skill, good looks, and an appealing personality—led Midland International to sign Travolta to a recording contract in 1976. His ballad, "Let Her In," went to #10 that June and led to two more small hits.

While Travolta wasn't a very good singer, he was a bankable actor, and *Saturday Night Fever* soon made him a mega-star. He and Olivia Newton-John (also just a bit too old to be playing a high schooler) co-starred in the film version of *Grease,* and the stars duetted on two major hits from the soundtrack: "You're the One that I Want" (#1) and "Summer Nights" (#5).

8. DAVID SOUL

David Soul is a multitalented performer. He was offered a pro baseball contract, but elected to begin an acting career in North Dakota in the early '60s. Soon inked to a talent contract, he was a bit player on TV shows from 1967 through the early '70s.

Soul eventually got his own series at age 34 when he and Paul Michael Glaser were selected to star in *Starsky and Hutch* in 1975. With the show's successful four-year run, Soul became something of a matinee idol and was signed by Private Stock records. His ballad, "Don't Give Up on Us," raced all the way to the top of the charts in early 1977.

Soul wasn't a one-trick pony; he actually recorded five albums, some of them overseas, and had more success as a singer in England than in the United States.

9. PATRICK SWAYZE

Red Dawn (1984) was veteran actor Swayze's first big success. After that, he did some TV miniseries work and was tabbed to star in *Dirty Dancing* in 1987. At age 35, he portrayed, fairly convincingly, a man in his early 20s beginning a relationship with a girl in her teens. Swayze was also asked to sing a song on the soundtrack album.

While "She's Like the Wind" was nothing special as a song or a production, it did reveal that Swayze had not-inconsiderable vocal talent. He and co-vocalist Wendy Fraser rode all the way to #3 with the song, which peaked on the charts in January 1988.

After co-starring with Demi Moore in the phenomenally successful *Ghost* in 1990, Swayze has been involved with a few smash movies and several outright bombs. He hasn't continued to make records.

10. DON JOHNSON

Johnson was a veteran actor who had done years of small parts after breaking into the movies in 1970. He finally got his big break in 1984 when he was picked to co-star as a two-day's-stubbled detective in *Miami Vice*. The oh-so-hip show, which also featured Philip Michael Thomas, made Johnson a star.

He originally began his professional career in musicals, and could sing well enough to make records. In 1986, Johnson struck gold with "Heartbeat," which went Top 5 on the charts. Two years later, he duetted with Barbra Streisand on a song from the musical, *Goya* ("Till I Loved You"), that was a smash on adult contemporary stations.

Since then, Johnson has continued to act in a range of films, few of which have done much, and he starred in TV's *Nash Bridges*. It's been a long time since he sang for a living. He'll need a late-career burst if he doesn't want to be remembered primarily for his two marriages to Melanie Griffith.

Old Time
Rock & Roll

No record any pop singer or group can release— *Pet Sounds, Revolver, OK Computer, What's Going On*—will ever fully satisfy lovers of classical music who believe that rock music is simply an abomination.

But plenty of rockers love the classics. (Some, like Elvis Costello, Paul McCartney, and Chris Stamey, have written symphonies and art songs.) As the following list shows, plenty of rockers know a good tune when they hear one. Sometimes, they even liked them enough to steal 'em.

1. "BUMBLE BOOGIE," B. BUMBLE AND THE STINGERS

An aggregation of sessionmen, including bluesmen/jazzers Earl Palmer and Plas Johnson, based this jangly-piano-led pop instrumental on the

Rimsky-Korsakov piece, "Flight of the Bumble-bee." Talk about a gimmick; the band's name obviously came *after* the record's concept was invented.

After "Bumble Boogie" was a surprise hit, reaching #21 in spring 1961, the formula was repeated the next year by this ad hoc session band, who cut "Nut Rocker," a takeoff on Tchaikovsky's *Nutcracker Suite* from his "Nutcracker" ballet.

B. Bumble and the Stingers also recorded "Bumble Bossa Nova," "Bee Hive," and "Dawn Cracker," but never had another hit.

2. "NIGHT," JACKIE WILSON

Wilson, who joined Billy Ward and the Dominoes in 1953 to replace departing superstar vocalist Clyde McPhatter, became a solo artist in 1957. His "Lonely Teardrops" was a Top 10 smash the following year.

However, by 1960 Wilson's career was foundering. He hadn't enjoyed another Top 10 hit, and his stock was sliding. Classical melodies to the rescue! His song, "Night," was based on Camille Saint-Saëns's "My Heart at Thy Sweet Voice" from the opera, *Samson and Delilah*.

This dramatic production became his biggest-ever hit, reaching #4 in April. Wilson's sweet voice and the record's over-the-top instrumentation were a natural match.

The formula was repeated twice more with great success. Later that year, "Alone at Last," based on a Tchaikovsky piano concerto, made the Top 10, as did 1961's "My Empty Arms," with a melody lifted from an aria from the opera, *I Pagliacci.*

The success enjoyed by these kinds of records made Wilson's late '60s switch to R&B that much more unexpected.

3. **"A WHITER SHADE OF PALE," PROCOL HARUM**

Five British lads, veterans of such R&B groups as The Paramounts, assumed a baffling new identity in 1967 as Procol Harum (poor Latin for "beyond these things").

In the heady atmosphere of London in the '60s, these fellows donned wildly psychedelic clothes, sang lyrics influenced by Bob Dylan, and based their rocking but often solemn music around a musical mix that was part Ray Charles and part Johann Sebastian Bach.

The new band's first release, "A Whiter Shade of Pale," was an international smash. It included a beautiful melody line, played by organist Matthew Fisher, styled on two Bach pieces: "Air on a G String" and "Sleepers Awake." Procol's first three albums featured Fisher and pianist/singer Gary

Brooker's unique mix of the bluesy and the churchy before Fisher departed in 1969.

4. "I LIE AWAKE," THE NEW COLONY SIX

This six-piece Chicago-area garage band had a small national hit with its first record, late 1965's "I Confess."

As was the practice in those days (and, some-times, *these* days), groups tried to make their second single sound like the first, to rope in those listeners who liked the song the first time around.

The NC6 copied the sound of "I Confess," reusing a guitar played through a Leslie speaker, an organ, a shuffling drumbeat, and a cascade of clever lyrics delivered in quick succession. To this, they added a melody lifted from George Gershwin's "Rhapsody in Blue" and came out with "I Lie Awake," more of a holding action than a hit.

The band's biggest chart successes—"I Will Always Think about You" and "Things I'd Like to Say"—were still years away.

5. "A LOVER'S CONCERTO," THE TOYS

Classical soul music made the charts in 1965 with this Spectoresque number cut in New York City.

The lyrics, about the simple joy of recognizing one's true love, were married to music from J.S. Bach's 17th-century "Minuet in G," also known as "Notebook for Anna Magdalena Bach."

The Toys, three young ladies who met in Jamaica, New York, enjoyed a #2 hit in the United States with the innovative disc and broke through to the Top 10 in Britain.

Sandy Linzer and Denny Randell, longtime pop songwriters, took credit for the song, which was the Toys' only Top 10 hit. After "Attack," a #18 charter in early 1966, the trio disappeared from the limelight.

6. "TOO YOUNG TO BE ONE," THE TURTLES

Buried on the second side of their 1967 *Happy Together* album, which included the #1 hit title track as well as its follow-up, "She'd Rather Be with Me," the Turtles recorded a song by then-little-known songwriter Warren Zevon, entitled "Too Young to Be One."

The only thing really memorable about the lightweight "Too Young to Be One" was its melody, which was lifted almost completely from an early Shaker devotional, "Simple Gifts," which 20th-century American composer Aaron Copland had previously melded into the masterpiece "Appalachian Spring."

7. "A SONG OF JOY," MIGUEL RIOS, AND "JOY," APOLLO 100

The final movement of Beethoven's *Ninth Symphony,* "Ode to Joy," is one of the world's most enduring pieces of music. It has been used in many pop contexts, including the Beatles' film, *Help!* and in the instrumental break of Elvis Costello's "The Only Flame in Town."

Twenty-six-year-old Spanish singer Miguel Rios penned new lyrics to the familiar tune and cut his adaptation in 1970. One of the first songs sung in a foreign language to become a major American hit, "A Song of Joy" reached #14. (It also topped the Australian charts in December of that year for three weeks.) Rios enjoyed more hits in Spanish-speaking countries and is credited with helping to develop the "Rock en Español" movement.

Two years later, British studio group Apollo 100 cut a frenetic, heavily orchestrated version of Beethoven's ode. Entitled "Joy," this disc featured bandleader Tom Parker playing intricate organ and harpsichord parts. "Joy," a memorable record, leapt all the way to #6 on the American charts in the summer of 1972.

8. "COULD IT BE MAGIC," BARRY MANILOW

In 1971, Barry Manilow was the lead singer of a group called Featherbed, who cut an album for Bell Records. One of the tracks was a Manilow song inspired by Frédéric Chopin's "Prelude in C Minor" titled "Could It Be Magic."

The album went nowhere, so Manilow was forced to get other gigs. He spent time as Bette Midler's accompanist, then wrote some jingles.

In 1974, he was signed as a solo artist. Manilow enjoyed his first hit with "Mandy," and his career took off. He recorded a new, more dramatic and orchestrated version of "Could It Be Magic" for 1975 release, and it became his third hit single, reaching the Top 10 that August.

9. "ALL BY MYSELF," ERIC CARMEN

After Carmen's band, the Raspberries, split in 1975, the band's lead singer decided to alter his style completely. No longer bound by his previous Beatles/Beach Boys pop-rock-harmony approach, Carmen wrote a lugubrious, romantic ballad, covered it in a melodramatic string arrangement, and draped it around a piano part swiped from Sergey Rachmaninoff's "Piano Concerto #2 in C minor." (Carmen didn't acknowledge the debt in the writing credits, however.)

"All by Myself" was a huge hit, reaching #2 on the *Billboard* charts. Next was "Never Gonna Fall in Love Again," a second affecting if overproduced ballad that photocopied another page from Rachmaninoff's book, this time from his second symphony. Carmen's single went to #11.

Carmen had more hits through the '90s, and Celine Dion's cover version of "All by Myself" was a smash in 1996. When Dion's version was released, however, Rachmaninoff was credited as co-writer.

10. "A FIFTH OF BEETHOVEN," WALTER MURPHY

The disco era produced its share of novelty records—Alec Constandinos's "Romeo and Juliet" and Meco's "Star Wars/Cantina Band" being particularly memorable—but Walter Murphy's "composition" was the biggest novelty disco hit.

Converting Beethoven's *Fifth Symphony* into a string-laden, dramatic dance-floor shouter with a jazzy electric piano solo, Murphy, a former jingle writer long infatuated with the idea of combining pop and the classics, reached #1 with his record in October 1976. The song was also featured in the blockbuster film, *Saturday Night Fever*.

Murphy's follow-up records, based on other classical pieces such as Gershwin's "Rhapsody in Blue" and Rimsky-Korsakov's "Flight of the Bumblebee," didn't chart.

Let's Get It On

Ladies and gentlemen, *please control your-selves!*

The following songs feature sounds and lyrics far more suited to the privacy of the bedroom than the airwaves, although most of these records received plenty of radio play in their day.

While we simply could have printed Prince's entire catalogue for this category ("Gett Off," "If I Was Your Girlfriend," "Erotic City," "Cream," etc.), we chose to widen our scope somewhat.

1. "OH, SUCH A NIGHT," ELVIS PRESLEY

Maybe it was the relief of getting out of the Army that helped release this, er, especially *masculine* side of Elvis.

After informing us unhelpfully in this 1964 Top 20 hit (recorded way back in 1960, a month after he got out of the service), "It was a night. Oh, yes, it really, really was. You know, it really was such a night," Elvis gets a bit more specific at the song's finish and tells us *why* it was such a night.

As the music builds to a rockin' crescendo, Elvis and his (male) backup singers act out just what that night might have sounded like from the Pelvis's point of view, groaning "oohs" and "aahs" that must have made every program director of the time blush.

2. "LOVELY RITA," THE BEATLES

Yes, even the Fabs got down and dirty in the grooves. Stuck in the middle of side two of the *Sergeant Pepper's Lonely Hearts Club Band* album was the charming "Lovely Rita," a Paul McCartney song about dating a meter maid.

At the song's end, the Beatles' crude brand of Liverpudlian humor came out. Over a jazzy and surprisingly dark piano interlude, John and Paul engage in some very rude and clearly orgasmic vocal interjections that suggest exactly what the guys' intentions were for the end of their evening with Rita.

This wasn't an isolated bit of fun; remember that in 1965's "Girl," the guys sang "tit tit tit" during the song's bridge, and that John Lennon would later master the orgasmic moan in songs like "Revolution 1." And then there was McCartney's line in "Penny Lane" about "fish and finger pie..."

Paul McCartney at his boyhood school, which later became the
Liverpool Institute for the Arts.

3. "ALL I WANNA DO," THE BEACH BOYS

The 1969 *20/20* album was one of the most varied the Beach Boys ever recorded. Mike Love's contribution was a hard rocker, "All I Wanna Do," in which he expressed his desire: "just wanna make some love to you."

For this number, Love took himself to a surprisingly wild place, singing words like, "You gave away everything you had, but there's one thing I want you to hold." His unusually no-holds-barred vocals, which climaxed in a maniacal scream buried unnecessarily in the mix, led into a postfadeout surprise—some "bedroom verité" recording featuring a squeaky bed and a moaning woman.

This from the clean-cut, striped-shirted guys from Hawthorne, California, who would later become Ronald Reagan's favorite band?

4. "JE T'AIME...MOI NON PLUS," SERGE GAINSBOURG AND JANE BIRKIN

French entertainer Serge Gainsbourg (1928–1991, born Lucien Ginzburg) first came to prominence in the '50s. A singer, songwriter, painter, and writer, he began his career half-singing his poems over beatnik jazz.

When rock invaded France in 1963, Gainsbourg realized he'd have to keep up. Already 35, he sang "Requiem for a Twister" and penned hits for Petula Clark, Marianne Faithfull, and Nana Mouskouri. He then hooked up with Brigitte Bardot and wrote the motorcycle anthem, "Harley Davidson," for her. Gainsbourg also wrote what he considered to be his first "real" love song, penning *"Je T'Aime . . . Moi Non Plus"* for Bardot.

The two recorded it in 1967 while making love in the studio, but Bardot got cold feet about the recording, asked that it not be released, and eventually left Gainsbourg. A year later, Gainsbourg met Jane Birkin, who was half his age—just 20—and convinced her to rerecord the song.

Sounding like Procol Harum's "Whiter Shade of Pale" playing during an orgy, the lovers' duet whispered, crooned, cooed, oohed, and aahed through lyrics more psychosexual than sexual. The title translates to "I love you . . . neither do I," and despite Birkin's orgasmic moaning, Gainsbourg sings about both pleasing his woman and holding back from her.

It was an instant smash all over the world, from Paris to Jamaica, but not one without its price. Gainsbourg and Birkin, always provocative figures in public, were held up as objects of ridicule and disgust. The president of Italy's Phonogram record company, which released "*Je T'Aime,*" was excommunicated by the Vatican. England's BBC wouldn't play the song, although it reached #1 on the charts. In America, it received scant radio exposure and didn't make the Top 40.

Current artists such as Air, Beck, and St. Etienne have acknowledged the tremendous debt they owe to the combination of '60s rock, theater, and poetry Gainsbourg created over his 35-year career.

5. "JUNGLE FEVER," THE CHAKACHAS

"Jungle Fever," as Spike Lee would inform the mass populace much later in a popular film, is slang for the Caucasian desire to experience the African-American sexual experience firsthand.

This 1972 Afro/Latin-influenced instrumental number, composed and played by a studio band from Belgium (!), featured exotic-sounding percussion and the standard "soul" sound of the day. Although it broke into the Billboard Top 10 in early 1972, "Jungle Fever" is one of the least-remembered hits of the last 30 years.

Perhaps that's because the record isn't played much on oldies radio. Why? Because "Jungle Fever" features the vocal interjections of an obviously aroused woman in the throes of an either intensely pleasurable or slightly painful (or both) physical encounter. These over-the-top vocal parts are more comical than sexy, though, because they are constantly being interrupted by a silly-sounding low trombone.

6. "PILLOW TALK," SYLVIA

Born in 1936, Sylvia Vanderpool was performing as "Little Sylvia" when she was 14. In 1957, she recorded the epochal "Love Is Strange" as half of Mickey and Sylvia (with singer and guitarist Mickey Baker). The song remains a rock standard.

Sylvia was a spry and randy 37-year-old in 1973 when her only solo hit, "Pillow Talk," reached #3 on the charts. Her sexy whispers of love and passion were evocative, especially for the time, and the record served as makeout music for plenty of kids and adults in the early seventies.

Eventually Sylvia married Joe Robinson, president of the Vibration label, which had released "Pillow Talk." Later, Joe founded Sugar Hill Records, and Sylvia Robinson was picked to serve as the artistic visionary of the pioneering rap record company.

7. "LOVE TO LOVE YOU, BABY," DONNA SUMMER

From its breathy opening, the nearly 17-minute epic, "Love to Love You, Baby," (chopped to three minutes-plus for AM radio play) was a hit. The slow disco high-hat cymbals, the wah-wah guitars, the sumptuous string arrangement, and Donna Summer's alternately celestial and down-and-dirty vocals were a magnet to record buyers.

As the music swelled, Summer moaned and groaned in orgasmic ecstasy. That sealed it—this was one of the most overtly sexual records ever made. It went all the way to #2 on the charts in December 1975, the first of Summer's 14 Top 40 hits.

The record was made in Germany, where Donna (born LaDonna Gaines) had journeyed to appear in a production of *Hair*. While there, she married actor Helmid Sommer (they later divorced).

Donna, whose handlers stressed that she had been raised as a Christian in a traditional family, was reportedly embarrassed by the attention given to the song and unhappy with her new image as a sex queen. However, such queasiness didn't stop her from posing as a prostitute, wearing a slip and standing on a street corner, for the cover of her 1979 *Bad Girls* album.

8. "ORGASM ADDICT," THE BUZZCOCKS

The early days of punk made room for all sorts of talented groups playing aggressive music with lyrics based on everyday life.

One such band was the Buzzcocks, whose name alone was guaranteed to raise hackles among England's self-appointed guardians of public morality. "Orgasm Addict," a standout early track, remains one of punk rock's enduring anthems.

Written by original group leader Howard Devoto and lead singer Pete Shelley, it wasn't a big hit, but became one of the Buzzcocks' best-known and most influential songs.

A furiously paced, catchy, one minute, 58-second number, "Orgasm Addict" featured Shelley breathing heavily, moaning, and yelping his way through a short instrumental passage presaging the song's bridge: "You're making out with school-kids, winos, and heads of state! You've even made it with the ladies who put the little plastic brownies [elves] on the Christmas cakes!"

q. "YOUR LOVE IS KING," SADE

Sade's debut album, 1985's *Diamond Life,* laid out the plans perfectly for world domination.

Featuring Sade Adu, a beautiful woman of mixed racial heritage blessed with a gorgeous voice, the British quartet's jazzy, soulful material could hardly lose.

"Your Love Is King," Sade's second single, was all about sex. And not subtly. "You're making me dance inside," the Nigerian/British vocalist declaimed over a backing led by an insistent, sultry saxophone riff. Sexy enough, yes, but the song's critical lyrical tag was "I'm coming up. I'm . . . coming."

This provocative line was repeated as the record faded into silence, leaving the listener with the image of Sade Adu coming.

10. "BUMP 'N' GRIND," R. KELLY

"My mind is telling me no . . . but my body's telling me YES! . . . Don't see nothin' wrong with a little bump and grind," sang the sexy Chicago-bred superstar on his second album, 1993's *12 Play*.

R. Kelly's combination of frank lyrics and well-produced, seductive music made him one of contemporary R&B's biggest stars. Recording first with Public Announcement, and later on his own, he took the group vocals of the New Jack Swing style and combined them with funk beats and sweetly soulful singing. "Bump 'n' Grind" remained #1 on the R&B charts for three months in 1994 and was a pop #1 for four weeks.

Kelly, who peppered *12 Play* with songs like "I Like the Crotch on You," "Your Body's Callin'," and "Sex Me," was quite the lover in real life as well. He married 15-year-old singer Aaliyah Houghton in 1994 and served as her musical mentor.

Chicago singer R. Kelly, whose smooth and sexy music has seduced a generation.

While his star has dimmed as other, younger, singers like Usher have tried to steal his thunder, Kelly's mojo still works. An entire generation of children has been conceived to his music.

Song to the Siren

Since the late 1960s, rock musicians have felt more comfortable writing "confessional" songs about their lives and thoughts. The rock & roll world being what it is, and relationships in a fairly small community being what they are, some of these songs have been about other rock stars. Bruce Johnston, for instance, penned "I Write the Songs" about his Beach Boys compatriot, Brian Wilson, and it became a worldwide #1 hit for an unlikely artist: Barry Manilow.

1. "SUITE: JUDY BLUE EYES," CROSBY, STILLS, AND NASH

The leadoff track on the trio's phenomenally successful 1969 debut album was a seven-minute-plus paean to Stills's former lover, folk/rock singer Judy Collins.

The two of them met in the late '60s, and he played on her *Who Knows Where the Time Goes* album. Their relationship was hot and volatile due to Collins's depression and Stills's own demons, which manifested themselves in this case in controlling behavior ("His idea of intimacy was my idea of bondage," Collins would later write).

Stills was able to channel his emotions into "Suite: Judy Blue Eyes," which has deservedly become one of FM radio's enduring mainstays. The poignant lyrics were matched by the tremendous close harmony singing of the group. The song certainly has lasted far longer than the relationship that inspired it.

2. "WILLY," JONI MITCHELL

After enjoying two successful albums, and seeing a flock of her songs covered by other artists, Joni Mitchell was a star by 1969. She started hanging around with the L.A. rock & roll in-crowd, which included at that time David Crosby, Steve Stills, and Graham Nash.

Stills played bass on Mitchell's first album, after which the long-legged blonde singer, already married and divorced, struck up a spark with Nash, formerly of the Hollies.

After an intense affair, the two parted. In writing tellingly and tenderly about him, she used her pet name for him, "Willy," which led to plenty of gossip and speculation. For his part, Nash noted that while it's wonderful to be involved with Joni Mitchell, there was one downside: the entire world might hear about it on her next album.

3. "TOO MANY PEOPLE," PAUL McCARTNEY

The battle between the two ex-Beatles reached an ugly peak in 1971. For his second solo album, *Ram,* McCartney chose to lead off with a catchy but bitter song about John Lennon and Yoko Ono, whom Paul felt were too arrogant and preachy for comfort.

"Too many people preaching practices/don't let 'em tell you what you wanna be," Paul and Linda McCartney sang. "That was your first mistake. You took your lucky break, and broke it in two," Paul continued, in a not-too-subtle reference to the Lennon-instigated bust-up of the Beatles.

The song itself began with Paul singing, "Piss off," another not-too-subtle dig at Lennon on an album whose sleeve featured a photo of one beetle mounting another. Several other songs on the homespun and somewhat banal album sported lyrics that most observers (including the Lennons) believed were addressed directly to John and Yoko.

4. "HOW DO YOU SLEEP?" JOHN LENNON

When Lennon was challenged, he rarely backed down.

Already angry at Paul McCartney for his post-Beatles lawsuit against the other three Fabs, and outraged by what he saw as the McCartneys' middle-class pomposity, Lennon heard digs at himself and his wife, Yoko Ono, in nearly every song on the *Ram* LP.

So Lennon decided to respond in kind. For the *Imagine* album, a disc split between tenderness and anger, the bitterest salvo by far was "How Do You Sleep?"

"Those freaks was right when they said you was dead," Lennon sang with palpable disdain. Weaving some of McCartney's song titles into the next line, he sneered, "The only thing you done was 'Yesterday,' and since you've gone, you're just 'Another Day.'" Subtle as a punch in the snout.

While the presence of George Harrison's caustic slide guitar solo intimated at least one other ex-Beatles' cooperation in the McCartney shredding, drummer Ringo Starr—always the most conciliatory of the Fab Four—more than once criticized John and George's mean-spiritedness during the sessions.

5. "THE JEAN GENIE," DAVID BOWIE

This was Bowie's salute to Iggy Pop, a hero to punks, metalheads, and glam rockers alike and a willing participant in the excesses of rock music.

Pop was lead singer of the wild, untamed Stooges in the late '60s (and was known as Iggy Stooge at the time). This was one of Detroit's rough-and-tumble bands, in the tradition of the MC5, which never quite broke commercially despite critical acclaim and a fanatical fan base.

In a song recorded in 1972 for the *Aladdin Sane* album, Bowie praised Pop's wildman behavior and humorously catalogued his excesses. Singing about a figure "Strung out on lasers and slashed-back blazers, ate all your razors while pulling the waiters," Bowie celebrated "The Jean Genie [who] lives on his back . . . he's outrageous, he screams and he bawls."

Pop and Bowie would remain friends and work together on various projects during their careers.

6. "ALEX CHILTON," THE REPLACEMENTS

"Children by the million wait for Alex Chilton," Paul Westerberg sang hopefully on this track from the 1987 album, *Pleased to Meet Me.*

A true believer in the power of a great pop song (having written several of them himself),

Westerberg imagined a world in which Chilton received due fame and fortune for his achievements.

Chilton, former lead singer of the Box Tops ("The Letter") and groundbreaking power-pop act Big Star, became a venerated hero to the American rock underground of the '80s. He had already contributed backup vocals to a song on the Replacements' previous album, *Tim*.

Despite the obvious affection that such '80s pop-rockers as the Replacements, the dBs, the Bangles, and R.E.M., have shown him, Chilton has rejected much of the cult attention afforded to his earlier bands. He prefers instead to concentrate on simple rock & roll tunes, old standards, and obscure R&B chestnuts.

7. "WE'RE THE REPLACEMENTS," THEY MIGHT BE GIANTS

For many people, the Replacements—a hard-partying, raucous band in the mode of punk bands and '70s stadium rock acts like Kiss and Aerosmith—would have little in common with brainy tunesmiths They Might Be Giants.

And maybe they don't. But TMBG, who often peppered their songs with references to current cultural figures (even mentioning '80s bands like the dBs and the Young Fresh Fellows in their song,

"Twisting"), released "We're the Replacements" in 1987.

The lyrics were written in a style reminiscent of the attitudes of an earlier time, supremely ironic considering the Replacements' well-known love of hard partying: "We're playing in a rock & roll band, rock & rolling until the break of dawn . . . moving equipment, where's the equipment? . . . Soon we're going home, then we'll have a party."

8. "BEER MONEY," THE YOUNG FRESH FELLOWS

When a famous American brewing company started sniffing around the alternative American bands of the mid '80s, it found bands like The Del Fuegos and The Long Ryders willing to go for the advertising dollar.

"Rock 'n' roll is just folk music. It's music for folks," said the Long Ryders in their beer commercial, which gained them plenty of negative publicity in the alternative rock press and didn't give them much exposure to the general public.

The Young Fresh Fellows, a band of pop-smart jokers from Seattle, chose to call a spade a spade, and in 1986 released "Beer Money," a sardonic song about the pitfalls of accepting advertising money while attempting to remain a grounded, small-scale rock group. (Of course, the Young Fresh Fellows had no trouble saying much of *anything,* once writing a song about Christian singer Amy Grant undressing.)

Ironically, Scott McCaughey of the YFF would later become an adjunct member of a larger aggregation, serving for several years in R.E.M.'s touring band and forming the Minus Five with the Georgia band's guitarist, Peter Buck, and former American Music Club singer Mark Eitzel.

9. "ELVIS IS EVERYWHERE," MOJO nIXON

"Elvis is everywhere, Elvis is everything, Elvis is everywhere, Elvis is still the king," sang rockin' wildman Mojo Nixon in a minor hit from 1987, asserting that "Everyone's got Elvis in them"—everyone except actor Michael J. Fox.

Nixon, who with percussionist Skid Roper formed a popular R&B duo in the early '80s, wasn't shy about targeting music-biz celebrities, penning and recording the derivative but entertaining "Debbie Gibson Is Pregnant with My Two-Headed Love Child," "Bring Me the Head of David Geffen," and "Don Henley Must Die."

Gibson wasn't happy about being immortalized in song, and the Geffen tune was pulled from the album shortly after its release, but at least

Henley showed some humor. He once actually took the stage with Nixon and accompanied him on the tune.

10. "HAPPY HERO," NEGATIVLAND

Brutally savage and possibly libelous, this song, almost certainly about Michael Jackson, appeared on the Bay Area noise/protest band's 1997 *Dispepsi* CD. The creative and often wildly funny *Dispepsi* is a concept affair about advertising, useless consumerism, and the control of the economy by a relative few.

Jackson, a longtime music industry wheel and Pepsi-Cola pitchman, as well as one of the most popular singers of his generation, is referred to several times on the CD. One reference is a news clip referring to Jackson's well-publicized injury when his hair caught fire while he was shooting a Pepsi commercial.

"Happy Hero" is a gruesome tale of a pathetic entertainer who weasels out of his problems (including child molestation, which Jackson has been accused of) with his charm, smile, and willingness to abase himself for any cause. The song ends with a singer being shot while filming a Pepsi commercial.

Rock & Roll Suicide

As the 1994 suicide of Kurt Cobain unnecessarily reminded us, many of music's greatest performers have been terribly unhappy. Some have conquered their problems and found peace. Others, however, took another way out.

1. RORY STORM

So close and so far... Rory Storm (born Alan Caldwell) was a well-regarded singer in Liverpool in the early '60s.

He had in his band, the Hurricanes, a popular local drummer named Ringo Starr. Had him, that is, until the Beatles asked him to join in 1961. While Storm didn't like it, he knew the Beatles were on their way, and it was only right to let Ringo do what he needed to do.

While other Merseyside groups cashed in after the Beatles hit it big, Rory Storm and the

Hurricanes didn't write many of their own songs, and couldn't bring their stage magic to disc. Storm never made it in music, and on September 27, 1972, shortly after his father died, he overdosed on painkillers. He was dead at 34.

2. **ALBERT AYLER**

Innovative free-jazz saxophonist Albert Ayler was a major influence on the avant-garde rock musicians of the '70s and '80s, including Sonic Youth, Eugene Chadbourne, and Pere Ubu, and, of course, countless jazz musicians.

Born in 1936, Ayler shared the anger felt by other black musicians in the '60s over how their culture was systematically ripped off by the entertainment establishment. This anger, as well as his own curious muse, drove his music further out of the mainstream, toward a rejection of all things standard and in search of a special beauty.

But he was also beset by family troubles. On November 25, 1970, Ayler, despondent over arguments with his mother about the mental problems of his brother and fellow musician, Donald, took the ferry to Brooklyn and jumped into the East River. He never came out.

Ayler had instructed friends earlier that his songwriting and record royalties were to be divided among the members of his family.

3. PETE HAM/TOM EVANS

Badfinger may have been the most cursed rock band ever.

After beginning their career as the Iveys, the four Welsh musicians hooked up with Paul McCartney and recorded his "Come and Get It" in 1969. However, this hit had its price, because the rechristened Badfinger (the name conceived by John Lennon) were considered Beatles wannabes. Despite their collective talent, Badfinger couldn't gain respect for their own abilities.

Their melodic but rocking pop gave them more American hits ("No Matter What," "Baby Blue," "Day After Day"), and Harry Nilsson enjoyed a big hit with their composition, "Without You."

However, crooked management kept the band from earning what they deserved. In addition, the struggles of their record label, Apple, led to a new deal with Warner Brothers, but the new label didn't treat Badfinger as a priority. Finally, there were interpersonal problems within the band. These three factors conspired to drive Badfinger underground too soon.

First to depart—permanently—was prodigiously talented singer/guitarist/keyboardist Pete Ham, who hung himself on April 24, 1975. He was morbidly depressed when he learned how he and the band had been ripped off by management, but probably had deeper problems as well.

While the rest of the group gamely tried to soldier on, bassist Tom Evans was scarred by Ham's death. He played on Badfinger's early '80s albums—*Say No More* and *Airwaves*—but gradually lost his sense of purpose. He also committed suicide, hanging himself in his garden on November 19, 1983.

In a grisly aside, Evans was rumored to have left a note for guitarist Joey Molland that read, "You're next."

4. PHIL OCHS

The well-known folksinger had fallen from favor in the early '70s. The causes Ochs fought for had already been lost, although the eventual end of the Vietnam War brought him out for a "The War Is Over" concert (he had also thrown an absurdist "War Is Over" party in 1967 as a protest).

Drinking far too much, and spinning into a cycle of depression, Ochs was isolated further when he was robbed in Africa. A mugging left him unable to sing for a period, and eventually his ability to write left him, too. On April 8, 1976, he hooked a belt onto a board at his brother's house in New York and slipped his neck in.

Many of Ochs's fans and friends would say that he really died in the late '60s, when his worst fears about America came true at the 1968 Democratic convention in Chicago. Ochs's 1969 album, *Rehearsals for Retirement,* featured on its front cover a gravestone that read: "Phil Ochs: born 1942, died 1968."

5. IAN CURTIS

As punk rock spread from London to the rest of England in 1977–78, bands from northern cities like Liverpool and Manchester began to sprout. Warsaw, a Manchester band, made some noise, but it took some new songs and a change in name—to Joy Division—to get on the map.

Early EPs and a debut album, *Unknown Pleasures,* laid out their basic sound: doomy, stark, and portentous. Some compared Joy Division to the Doors, but the band was all English, from its artsy visuals to its Bowiesque self-consciousness.

But just as Joy Division began to break through, and as American college radio began to embrace the band, Curtis decided to end it all. Two days before the group was scheduled to leave for a U.S. tour, he hung himself in his house on May 18, 1980. He hadn't even turned 24.

The posthumous single, "Love Will Tear Us Apart," and the album, *Closer,* established the no-longer-extant Joy Division as one of Britain's top bands, and the Factory record label as a prime finder of new talent.

None of Curtis's bandmates had any idea that their creative force was as miserable as his pose and lyrics might have indicated, and no one has ever figured out what illness or depression drove him to end his own life.

Having nothing else to do but continue, the other three members of the group—Bernard Sumner, Peter Hook, and Steven Morris—recruited keyboardist Gillian Gilbert and formed New Order. In that enigmatic group, as much a product of disco as punk, the four would enjoy unimagined success.

6. DONNY HATHAWAY

The emotive soul singer was well known in the industry for his interesting treatments of jazzy soul material. However, he was best known by the public for two major hits recorded with fellow Atlantic Records vocalist Roberta Flack, whom he had met at Howard University in the early '60s.

Flack and Hathaway's two big hits, 1972's "Where Is the Love?" and 1978's "The Closer I Get to You," remain standards, two of the most beautiful duets recorded in the last 40 years.

Hathaway also enjoyed some solo success, singing the theme song to the TV series, *Maude*.

However, Hathaway, who at one time had considered entering the ministry, was racked by doubts about his place in the world and was hospitalized at least once for depression. On January 13, 1979, Hathaway threw himself from the 15th floor of New York's Essex House hotel. His hotel room door was locked from the inside, and the window glass carefully removed.

7. DEL SHANNON

In late 1960, 21-year-old carpet salesman Del Shannon (born Charles Westover) and his keyboardist, Max Crook, wrote the song, "Runaway," and arranged it for guitar and musitron (a bizarre electric organ). The song was recorded in New York and raced up the charts in spring 1961. Finally reaching #1 for a month in April, the song made Shannon a star.

A significant talent with an original sound, Shannon enjoyed eight Top 40 hits overall between 1961 and 1965, including "Hats Off to Larry" and the dramatic "Keep Searchin'." He also wrote "I Go to Pieces," later a huge hit for Peter and Gordon. Shannon continued to write and moved into production in the late '60s and '70s.

A 1981 album, *Drop Down and Get Me,* produced by Tom Petty, made some noise for Shannon, and his version of the chestnut, "Sea of Love," made the Top 40. Shannon gained further acclaim by singing on Petty's 1989 *Full Moon Fever* LP. (One tune on the album, "Running Down a Dream," references Shannon and "Runaway.")

However, Shannon wasn't well. Suffering from alcoholism and depression for much of his life, he shot himself on February 8, 1990, bringing his life, and an underrated career, to a close.

8. RICHARD MANUEL

The Band remain one of the most beloved American rock bands. Their best records, 1968's *Music from Big Pink* and 1969's *The Band,* featured outstanding ensemble playing, strange lyrics, and a textured blend of sound that depended heavily on Richard Manuel's piano and voice.

Manuel, unfortunately, was the first member of the Band to get heavily into drugs and alcohol, and he blew himself out quickly. (He later said, "I became a party star. In fact, I became a party!") His sharp decline is one reason the group's later albums didn't have much of an impact.

During the '80s, after the Band broke up, Manuel didn't do much, which was probably the best thing for his health. When the Band reunited and began touring again in 1983, Manuel fell back into excessive drinking and drugging; that, plus the loss of expected income from his publishing rights, sent him into a dark place. Manuel hung himself in a hotel room following a show in Winter Park, Florida, on March 4, 1986.

9. DOUG HOPKINS

The Tempe, Arizona, music scene hadn't produced much since the days of Alice Cooper, but the Gin Blossoms changed that in the early '90s.

Songwriter/guitarist Doug Hopkins's catchy songs and the five-piece band's rootsy, melodic rock got the group a contract with A&M in 1990. When their first LP, *New Miserable Experience,* hit the stores in 1991, radio and MTV jumped all over singles "Hey, Jealousy" and "Found Out about You," sad-sack tales of drinking, regret, and occasional salvation written by the clinically depressed Hopkins.

But Hopkins was living the life he wrote about, drinking far too much, poisonous behavior for anyone suffering from depression. The rest of the band claimed he was too wiped out to play effectively, even in the studio, and he was hard to work with. While all involved acknowledged that alcohol was an issue, Hopkins felt that the others exaggerated his problems to create a power struggle.

Hopkins was kicked out in April 1992, even though nobody else in the band was a songwriter. Lead singer Robin Wilson and guitarist Jesse Valenzuela took over some of the writing chores, and the Gin Blossoms also brought in outside songwriters like Marshall Crenshaw in an attempt to recreate Hopkins's muse.

While Hopkins played with some pickup groups around Tempe, he sank lower when the rest of the Blossoms sued him to change their royalty arrangements. Hopkins shot himself to death on December 5, 1993. The Gin Blossoms' second album didn't sell, and the band slipped from view.

10. WENDY O. WILLIAMS

The punk movement led to plenty of bands with flash but not much else to recommend them. The Plasmatics were one of those acts, featuring singer Wendy O. Williams, the first prominent woman in rock to wear a mohawk.

The upfront and caustic Williams often took the stage wearing nothing but the bottom half of a bikini and two strips of carefully placed surgical tape. The band peppered their stage show with acts like chain-sawing instruments, smashing television sets, and even blowing up cars.

After the band's 15 minutes of fame ran out, Williams recorded three solo albums and played with Ultrafly and the Hometown Girls.

A noted animal lover, Williams spent the last years of her life acting, writing, and taking care of wild animals in the forests near her home in Connecticut. But on April 6, 1988, despondent over the "hypocrisies of the world," she shot herself.

Rock & Roll Stew

When rock music became truly big business in the late '60s, star power became a way to secure recording contracts, concert tours, and TV appearances.

The supergroup phenomenon—combining already well-known talents in specially constructed bands or short-term joint projects—continues to this day despite its questionable artistic or financial success.

But the occasional successes led to more opportunities. As the Steve Stills/Mike Bloomfield "Super Session" self-indulgence of 1968 to the awful 2001 version of "Lady Marmalade" by a bunch of disposable pop-ettes demonstrated, we're certainly not done with supergroups.

1. CREAM

After quitting the Yardbirds (whom he thought were too "pop") in 1965, guitarist Eric Clapton played with bluesman John Mayall, then took some time to rethink his direction.

Clapton wanted to play with like-minded professionals, hoping to emulate heroes like Buddy Guy and Albert King while playing with a visionary, interesting rhythm section. He found drummer Ginger Baker and bassist Jack Bruce in Manfred Mann's band, and the three joined as Cream in 1966.

Baker, influenced by African rhythms, used extra emphasis on his tom-toms, while Bruce played a novel six-string bass. Clapton outfitted himself with guitar effects and played *loud*. The experimental playing was wed to traditional blues structures and some strange original songs featuring odd, stream-of-consciousness lyrics. Poet Pete Brown collaborated with Bruce on some songs.

After a lightweight first single, the poppy, '20s-ish "Wrapping Paper," the group's debut LP, *Fresh Cream*, outlined the direction—loud, rocking, bluesy, and, at times, oddly sloppy.

But by mid-1967, the band was moving from blues progressions with weird lyrics to more original constructions. The second Cream LP, *Disraeli*

Gears, featured Bruce's riff-based "SWLABR" and "Sunshine of Your Love" and Clapton's wah-wah-fest, "Tales of Brave Ulysses," three tracks that helped to define psychedelic blues and heavy metal.

But cracks were appearing. In concert, Cream—all three convinced of their star quality—were prone to 20-minute jamming, the odd energy and strange tunefulness of the studio lost. While the pyrotechnics and flash won them some additional fans, they also helped to destroy the group's chemistry by emphasizing soloing, an individual act, rather than a group dynamic. The half-live, half-studio double LP, *Wheels of Fire,* emerged in 1968. Along with the hit, "White Room," came the live, "Crossroads," their most famous concert song.

Cream broke up in early 1969, leaving behind a skimpy album, *Goodbye,* padded with more concert material. Why did Cream evaporate? Bruce was no favorite of the other two because of his domineering style, and Clapton was going through personal problems having to do with women and drugs.

In retrospect, Cream was doomed to fail. Each member of the group, already well established in the public's eye, wanted to be the centerpiece, and the three had no friendship to keep them together during the ensuing conflicts.

2. JEFF BECK GROUP

Beck, like Clapton, was a refugee from the Yardbirds. He, too, wanted to play in a band. His 1967 solo hits, "Hi Ho Silver Lining" and "Love Is Blue," left him unsatisfied.

In 1968, he formed the Jeff Beck Group with bassist Ron Wood, pianist Nicky Hopkins, and drummer Aynsley Dunbar (who soon left in favor of Mickey Waller). Rod Stewart, formerly of the three-lead-vocalist act, Steampacket, was recruited to sing.

Beck, whose reputation was that of a prodigiously talented guitar player with poor self-discipline and a checkered personal history, held things in place for the *Truth* and *Beck-Ola* albums, two bellwethers of heavy rock in 1968–69. On one track, "Beck's Bolero," future Led Zeppelin members Jimmy Page and John Paul Jones played rhythm guitar and bass, and the Who's Keith Moon supplied the drums.

Beck and Stewart contributed few original songs, but did a good job on contemporary material by others, including the Impressions' "People, Get Ready" and "Shapes of Things" (originally recorded by Beck with the Yardbirds in 1966).

For the first time, Stewart was able to let loose in a high-profile situation, and, ultimately, the JBG's success did more for his career than it did for Beck's. The two stars didn't like each other, and their uneasy alliance finally exploded in late 1969. Wood and Stewart joined Faces after Steve Marriott left the group to form Humble Pie. Beck tried, with a nonsuperstar lineup, to rekindle the Jeff Beck Group in 1971, but two poor albums resulted.

3. THE SOUL CLAN

The soul musicians of the American South knew just how lucky they were in the '60s. Most had come from lower-middle-class backgrounds or worse and had no desire to leave their communities behind.

As singer/songwriter Solomon Burke told Rhino Records a few years ago, "With the end of segregation, nobody thought about the negative impact on black-owned businesses. Who's gonna stay at the run-down black motel when now you can stay at the Holiday Inn down the street? The people in the South, who were running those motels, living in shacks, were our fans. They had our records. We had a responsibility to them."

Therefore, Burke, Don Covay (writer of "Chain of Fools"), Joe Tex ("Skinny Legs and All"), Wilson

Pickett, and Otis Redding came together to form the Soul Clan. This group of singers, most of them signed to Atlantic Records, would procure an advance from the label to record an album. Then they would use the advance to build affordable housing and improve the business infrastructure in Memphis's black community.

Unfortunately, Redding's death in an airplane crash on December 10, 1967, which shattered the soul scene, scuttled the project. With the biggest star of the group gone, Pickett decided to take a pass on the Soul Clan project. To make things worse, Atlantic wouldn't pay the $1 million advance the quintet had originally requested.

However, Atlantic did agree to fund a single. With Arthur Conley ("Sweet Soul Music") and Ben E. King ("Stand By Me") as replacements for Redding and Pickett, the Soul Clan cut "Soul Meeting" and "That's How It Feels," two sides of classic gospel-tinged, greasy southern soul.

The single bombed out, however, reaching only #91 on *Billboard* in July 1968. The Soul Clan dissolved.

In 1981, the Soul Clan came back. This time, Pickett was happy to join Covay, Burke, King, and Tex. They did a few shows and enjoyed some success, but Tex's death the following year ended the group's run. King, Covay, and Pickett were pall-bearers at Joe Tex's funeral.

4. CROSBY, STILLS, NASH, AND YOUNG

The supergroup that defined the term gestated in California. Where else?

Graham Nash of the Hollies, envying the vibes of the American west coast and feeling distanced from his pop-oriented British bandmates, vacationed in California in 1968 and met Steven Stills and David Crosby.

Having been ejected from the Byrds, Crosby was looking for a chance to reestablish himself. Stills, whose group, Buffalo Springfield, had imploded that same year, had been cooling his heels and writing songs, preparing for a solo project.

When Stills and Crosby sang with Nash (whose vocals they had admired from the Hollies days), all three were amazed at the resulting harmonies. The trio went into songwriting and rehearsals, with Atlantic Records, which had signed them, alerting the rock press that something was brewing.

By the time the album, *Crosby, Stills, and Nash,* emerged in spring 1969, the buzz was palpable. The record became a major hit. The first single, Stills's "Suite: Judy Blue Eyes," his valentine to paramour Judy Collins, was a smash on both AM and FM, as was the follow-up, Nash's "Marrakesh Express."

Despite augmenting their sound with drummer Dallas Taylor, CS&N needed some fleshing out for live performances. Stills's former bandmate, Neil Young, was asked to join, although the two had been frequent and bitter combatants in Buffalo Springfield.

The renamed Crosby, Stills, Nash, and Young recorded one studio album, *Déjà Vu,* another smash hit, and a mediocre live LP, *4-Way Street,* before Young departed for solo stardom. The "band" dissolved after recording Young's Kent State elegy, "Ohio."

Crosby, Stills, and Nash (with and without Young) played in various combinations over the years but were never again relevant. Even their original fans tired of their moribund solo projects and reunion rumors, especially after CSN's once-novel acoustic guitar and harmony vocals approach became the norm, rather than the exception, in the '70s.

5. BLIND FAITH

One would have thought the lessons of Cream would have taught Eric Clapton and Ginger Baker something.

But no! Instead of going their separate ways, or playing with some other, more obscure musicians, the two hooked up with another established star— this time former Traffic singer/multi-instrumentalist Steve Winwood—as well as ex-Family bassist Rik Grech in early 1969. This aggregation was presciently named Blind Faith.

This new band was supposed to allow Clapton and Winwood to get their songs out without the pressures of dealing with their former bands. The pair's stardom was also a way to ensure immediate public and critical attention.

But while Crosby, Stills, and Nash had spent months getting their sound together and hanging out, Clapton, Winwood et al. were shoved into the limelight immediately. They recorded an album in a matter of weeks and were sent on a huge English and American tour (their first show was played to 100,000 people) in the summer of 1969.

While their self-titled album has some good songs, such as "Can't Find My Way Home" and "Presence of the Lord," the group never had time to develop into an organic unit. Audience demands for endless soloing made Clapton miserable, and the still-new foursome played its last show August 26, 1969.

Clapton hooked up with Delaney and Bonnie, who had been the tour's support act, while

Winwood eventually retreated back to England and began recording a solo album that would become Traffic's classic *John Barleycorn Must Die.*

6. ROCKPILE

Dave Edmunds, a star in the U.K. since his days in the late '60s with the trio, Love Sculpture, spent much of the '70s recording his own music. However, he also produced bands like Flamin' Groovies and pub-rock stalwarts Brinsley Schwarz.

The latter-named band's bass player, Nick Lowe, an ambitious and likable character, struck up a friendship with Edmunds, and the two began to collaborate on records and live performances. Lowe himself became a producer, most notably of Elvis Costello's first recordings, and won a solo contract.

Lowe and Edmunds found friendly sidemen. Drummer Terry Williams, formerly of British hippie band Mud, provided the bashing, while talented, unassuming guitarist Billy Bremner filled out the sound.

The four played together on Edmunds and Lowe's records, and given the success that both achieved, it was only a matter of time before Rockpile (the name taken from Edmunds's 1972 debut LP) became a real live band.

The 1980 album, *Seconds of Pleasure,* contained songs from both Lowe and Edmunds, a song from Squeeze's Glenn Tilbrook and Chris Difford, and some well-chosen covers. A bonus disc of Lowe and Edmunds singing Everly Brothers classics was also included in some copies of the album, a clever and rocking mix of '50s and '60s influences, raucous rhythms, and good songwriting.

Rockpile were quite popular and appeared on ABC's *Fridays* show (which also featured exciting performances from such bands as The Clash, The Jam, and Devo during its short life). After a U.S. tour, however, the band broke up amid serious bickering between Lowe and Edmunds.

Bremner went on to play sessions, contributing the memorable guitar lines on the Pretenders' 1983 "Back on the Chain Gang" single, while Williams took the drummer's chair for a time in Dire Straits.

It took seven years for the foursome to record again, with 1987's unsatisfying *The Original Rockpile Part II* the result.

7. POWER STATION

Andy and John Taylor (not related) of Duran Duran were feeling their oats after their band's huge success and, in 1985 chose to try the solo route, teaming up with friend Robert Palmer.

Palmer, a 35-year-old veteran of the wars who had enjoyed hits back in the late '70s, was producing artists as diverse as reggae legend Desmond Dekker and Tangerine Dream keyboardist Peter Baumann. He welcomed the chance to get back in the ring and, with drummer Tony Thompson, formerly of Chic, Power Station recorded a self-titled album. Chic's producer, Bernard Edwards, produced the record.

Power Station spawned two American Top 10 hits: "Some Like It Hot" and a cover of T. Rex's anthem, "Get It On," were all over the airwaves in 1985.

The success of the album surprised everyone, and a tour was booked. Palmer, who was recording a solo album, declined to go on the road with Power Station, and Michael Des Barres, formerly lead singer of Chequered Past, was drafted.

His career reinvigorated, Palmer soon released the *Riptide* album and scored two massive hits: "Addicted to Love" and "I Didn't Mean to Turn You On," finally becoming a star after more than a decade in the biz.

Following their successful world tour, Power Station disbanded, with the Taylors returning to Duran Duran. It's a good thing they did; apparently, the massive sex and drugs the Taylors were said to have indulged in at the time could have killed them.

8. TRAVELING WILBURYS

In the late '80s, a like-minded set of star musicians began to work together in California, first on a George Harrison b-side and then, almost accidentally, deciding to form a group.

Each of the five already-famous members (Bob Dylan, George Harrison, Roy Orbison, Tom Petty, and former ELO mastermind Jeff Lynne) took on false names and false personas (Lefty Wilbury, Otis Wilbury, etc.). In 1987, augmented by legendary drummer Jim Keltner, the quintet unleashed *Traveling Wilburys, Volume I*.

The songs were well sung and well played, and the deliberately low-profile, handmade quality of the record (and its supporting videos) was charming. The "band" was a great idea, a way for each of five diverse talents to sing a few songs without the pressure of supporting an entire album. "Handle with Care," an outstanding single, featured Harrison and Orbison, but all five sang on it.

Following the release of the first album, Roy Orbison died of a heart attack on December 6, 1988. The video for the Wilburys' second single— "End of the Line"—featured the four survivors playing in a moving train; an empty rocking chair indicated Orbison's spectral presence.

The second album, *Volume III,* was released in 1990. It sounded a bit more tossed-off and not as catchy, despite some worthy tracks, including "Wilbury Twist," and did not sell nearly as well as a result. While some in the press bandied about names such as Donovan and Roger McGuinn as possible replacements for Orbison, the Wilburys remained retired.

9. CONTINENTAL DRIFTERS

Originally a trio that included Carlo Nuccio, Ray Ganucheau, and Mark Walton (formerly of the L.A. psychedelic band, Dream Syndicate), the Drifters became a quintet with the addition of Dan McGough and Gary Eaton.

However, the band, which formed in Los Angeles in 1991, was a loose and friendly aggregation often augmented by others who brought along their guitars.

Many of these friends were well known, including Peter Holsapple, formerly of the critically acclaimed dBs, singer Susie Cowsill (yes, the youngest of the '60s family group, The Cowsills, who recorded "The Rain, the Park, and Other Things"), and guitarist Vicki Peterson of the Bangles.

Eventually, Holsapple and Cowsill were wed, and they and Peterson joined the band, which set up shop in New Orleans. McGough, Ganucheau, and Eaton soon left, and the Continental Drifters (also briefly known as the Walkin' Tacos) filled out with guitarist Robert Maché, who had played with onetime Dream Syndicate singer/guitarist Steve Wynn. Drummer Nuccio departed and was replaced by Russ Broussard.

Since their first LP in 1994, the Continental Drifters have released three recordings, the newest studio one 2001's *Better Day*. The band puts on an excellent live show, mixing original songs with ones originally sung by Michael Nesmith, Dusty Springfield, Gram Parsons, and the Box Tops.

Holsapple and Cowsill have since divorced but remain bandmates. Peterson has taken some time off to work with the reunited Bangles, but remains a Continental Drifter.

10. GORILLAZ

A cartoon band formed around the contributions of some famous musicians, Gorillaz came into almost being in 2000.

Based on the contributions of Blur vocalist/keyboardist Damon Albarn, Cibo Matto singer Miho Hatori, rapper Del Tha Funkee Homosapien, DJ Dan "The Automator" Nakamura, and former

Talking Heads rhythm section Chris Frantz and Tina Weymouth, Gorillaz exist only as a cartoon concept.

While the project was viewed first as an Albarn solo CD, it turned into something wholly other. The music ranges from rap, trip-hop, and hip-hop to art rock, punk, and indie pop. Vocals from Albarn, Hatori, Del, and Cuban ballad singer Ibrahim Ferrer threw more ingredients into what was already a strange soup.

The CD was a surprise commercial and critical hit in 2001, with the single, "Clint Eastwood," garnering attention and airplay. At least this virtual band found a way to make the supergroup concept work—by not actually existing.

The Stroke

There have been songs about sex, even truly dirty ones, since the art of song began thousands of years ago. Rock music has been an outlet for creative, disgusting, funny, salacious, and exciting songs about sex—but not very many touching (pardon the pun) on the subject of solo sex. However, the following artists found creative and, sometimes, quite affecting ways to discuss the art of self-pleasure.

1. "CAPTAIN JACK," BILLY JOEL

Writing about cocaine on his 1973 *Piano Man* album, Joel illustrates the sad life of a young man who wants to do nothing more than stay high all the time.

Before going down to the city to look at the "drag queens," the song's protagonist has a typical night: "Your sister's gone out; she's on a date.

You just sit at home and masturbate." (Lloyd Cole would write later about masturbation and cocaine on his track, "My Bag," in 1987.)

"Captain Jack" is one of Joel's most honest and direct songs; by the time he reached his second career peak, in 1977, he was writing far less interesting material about far less edgy people and subjects.

2. "EVERYDAY I DIE," GARY NUMAN AND THE TUBEWAY ARMY

From the 1978 *Tubeway Army* album, "Everyday I Die" boasts some of the saddest lyrics in rock music. The frankness and brutality of the song is still surprising, considering that, at least visually, Numan has presented (and been credited with) an image of being cold, emotionless, and robotic.

The little death of the orgasm is Numan's subject in "Everyday I Die." His lyrics couldn't be more clear: "The problems of need. I need you. Obscene dreams in rusty beds. No one came here. Tonight I pulled on me; I need to. I unstick pages and read, I look at pictures of you. I smell the lust in my hands. Everyday I die."

3. "FOOLING YOURSELF," STYX

While some would accuse this Chicago-based band of an extended period of *musical* masturbation, the interpretation of Tommy Shaw's "Fooling Yourself (The Angry Young Man)" as an ode to self-pleasure requires some reading between the lines.

At the time of the song's release as a single (1978), some listeners referred to Shaw's composition as "Feeling Yourself," citing the chorus's lyrics as evidence: "*Come on.* Get back on your feet. You're the one they can't *beat,* and you know it. Come on, let's see what you've got. Just *give your best shot and don't blow it.*"

There are just too many risqué lines there for comfort.

4. "THE BEAT," ELVIS COSTELLO

The bespectacled one's ode to nascent sexuality, and its inherent traumas, appeared on 1979's *This Year's Model.* His second album, and his first with the Attractions, *TYM,* was a major artistic leap.

"The Beat" featured the chorus, "Have you been a good boy? Never played with your toy? Though you never enjoy, such a pleasure to employ."

While Costello avers in the second verse that "It takes two to tango," he pulls back from contact in the final verse, telling his love-to-be, "I keep thinking about your mother. I don't want to lick them. I don't want to be your lover; I just want to be your victim."

5. "TOUCHING ME, TOUCHING YOU," SQUEEZE

Still in their early new-wave era incarnation as five clever, rascally South London lads, Squeeze put this ode to the stroke on their second album, 1978's *Cool for Cats:* "I'm always touching myself; I've got nothing else to do. And when I'm touching myself, I'm always thinking of you."

While Glenn Tilbrook would sing plenty of Chris Difford's sexually oriented lyrics over the band's 20-year career, he would never again sing words so juvenile. By Squeeze's third album, the band's songwriting had grown up, and the boys were singing about marriage, careers, and babies.

6. "SHE BOP," CYNDI LAUPER

On her 1984 debut album, *She's So Unusual,* Lauper sang frankly about the female act of self-pleasure, a topic not often visited by pop musicians.

Lauper's lyrics dealt not only with the act of masturbation, but also with the religious guilt involved. "I hope He will understand," she sang, obviously worried about God's reaction to her constant "mess[ing] with the danger zone."

The third of an amazing five singles from *She's So Unusual* to reach the Top 40, "She Bop" went all the way to #3 in the summer of 1984. It's surely the biggest hit ever about masturbation.

Lauper would continue to sing about sex; her final Top 10 hit was 1989's steamy "I Drove All Night." The song's video featured images of cars on highways projected over Lauper's naked body.

7. "DARLING NIKKI," PRINCE

This standout track on 1984's *Purple Rain* saw The Artist Known at That Time as Prince meeting up with a sex professional who likes to "grind grind grind grind grind."

Nikki first makes our hero's acquaintance in a hotel lobby, "masturbating with a magazine." (Unfortunately, we never find out where this hotel is.) From this auspicious beginning, Prince accompanies Nikki to her "castle" and is amazed by the inventory of sex toys she possesses.

In a reverse "Norwegian Wood"-style ending, Prince wakes up the next morning to find his Darling Nikki gone, probably to "grind grind grind grind grind" with some other sucker.

8. "ST. SWITHIN'S DAY," BILLY BRAGG

A man masturbates to the thoughts of an old girl-friend, perhaps with a Polaroid picture of her in front of him.

While this may not be a particularly appealing thought to ponder, Billy Bragg somehow turned it into a beautiful love song: "With my own hands, when I make love to your memory, it's not the same; I miss the thunder, I miss the rain," Bragg sang, in his unaffected plainsman's voice, to the accompaniment of a solitary electric guitar on the 1984 album, *Brewing Up with Billy Bragg*.

9. "I TOUCH MYSELF," THE DIVINYLS

From Cyndi Lauper's heartfelt ode to the dizziness of teenage sexual impulses, we go to the other spectrum of the female act of self-love.

By 1991, Australia's Divinyls had 10 years together with little success to show for them. Band members began dropping out until only singer Christina Amphlett and guitarist/songwriter Mark McEntee were left.

As a result, what did they have to lose by writing a lyrically risqué and musically vapid piece of fluff? "I don't want anybody else . . . when I think about you, I touch myself. I really do," Amphlett cooed.

"I Touch Myself" came out in early 1991 and, aided by a graphic video, raced into the Top 10 in both America and England. This might have been a calculated bid for the mainstream, but it worked;

the Divinyls were famous, at least for a month or two.

10. "ICICLE," TORI AMOS

It's just a typical Easter morning at the Amos household, one in which young Tori finds herself alone in her room masturbating in her pumpkin-colored pajamas while the family sings religious songs downstairs.

"And when my hand touches myself, I can finally rest my head. And when they say 'take of His body' I think I'll take from mine instead," sings Amos, noting, as her eyes roll back in her head, that the Bible doesn't mention anything about *this* kind of holiness. Who exactly is she thinking of? God? Jesus? Some guy from down the street? That isn't clear, but it is intriguing.

"Icicle" is found on Ms. Amos's 1994 album, *Under the Pink*. Of course.

Both Sides Now

The following artists not only could engineer and produce records for others, they also chose to make musical statements of their own. Some of them enjoyed big-time success on the performing side; others found being in back of the recording console to be more profitable.

1. HOLLAND/DOZIER/HOLLAND

Singer Eddie Holland enjoyed a Top 40 hit, "Jamie," on Berry Gordy's Anna label in 1962. He soon moved into songwriting and production with his brother, Brian, and their friend, Lamont Dozier, on Gordy's Tamla/Motown label.

Bingo! The staggering list of classics from 1964 to 1970 written and produced by the three includes "You Keep Me Hangin' On," "Heat Wave," "Reach Out, I'll Be There," "Where Did Our Love Go?" "I'll Be There," "Can I Get a Witness?" "Nowhere to

Run," "Jimmy Mack," and "Baby, I Need Your Lovin'."

Trouble was brewing, however. The three wanted a bigger piece of the action and departed Motown in 1968 to form their own labels, Invictus and Hot Wax. They also wanted to perform.

While the new labels enjoyed some big hits (such as Freda Payne's "Band of Gold,") Holland/Dozier/Holland lacked Motown's marketing muscle and didn't have the first-rate talent to perform their songs that they'd had back at Berry Gordy's shop. In turn, Motown suffered as the classic songs provided by H/D/H disappeared.

While none of the three enjoyed the level of success as solo artists that he had as Motown writers and producers, Lamont Dozier did enjoy two Top 40 hits in 1974: "Trying to Hold on to My Woman" and "Fish Ain't Bitin'." In addition, Eddie Holland recorded "Leaving Here" in 1969, viewed today as a classic "Northern Soul" track.

The three currently run their own recording conglomerate, HDH Records, as well as five sublabels, including the still-active Invictus and Hot Wax.

2. THE STRANGELOVES

Three record men from New York, Bob Feldman, Jerry Goldstein, and Richard Gottehrer, had success writing and producing songs for the Angels ("My Boyfriend's Back") in 1963 and the McCoys in 1965 ("Hang On, Sloopy") before deciding to get in on the action themselves.

The three donned outlandish costumes and posed as Giles, Miles, and Niles Strangelove, three sheepherding brothers from Australia who developed a prize breed, the Gottehrer, which they registered with the Feldman-Goldstein company. Very clever.

Also clever were their songs, including the 1965 Top 20 classic, "I Want Candy" (covered by many bands, notably Bow Wow Wow in 1982); a pounding slab of rock, "Night Time"; and another slice of rock, "Hide and Seek," which they released under yet another group name—the Sheep. Reasons for the trio's woolly fetish remain unknown.

Gottehrer would continue producing into the '80s, manning the board for Blondie's first album and doing the same for the first two records by the Go-Gos. His authentic feel for classic '60s production styles helped both bands refine their attack.

3. GARY USHER

Usher was present at the birth of surf music, almost single-handedly fueled the hot-rod music craze, and helped produce some of psychedelic rock's highest highs. Despite this, he is unjustifiably neglected.

In 1960, he released his first record, "Driven Insane." By 1962, Usher had co-written the Beach Boys' "Surfin' Safari" and "409" and, soon after, was writing, producing, and playing on a baffling array of records. He wrote for the Hondells, Frankie Avalon, Dick Dale, Wayne Newton, and the Castells; produced the Honeys and the Astronauts; and teamed with Roger Christian to release several records of drag racing and hot-rodding music.

As an artist, Usher released records under various group names, but rarely enjoyed solo success; it seemed that his most influential work was to be done in the background. He helped get the Beach Boys signed to Capitol Records, and his work helped countless other young bands and artists to get their songs heard.

By the mid-'60s, Usher knew that surf and car music were finished, so he moved toward more progressive rock music, producing singles for garage legends like the Sons of Adam and folk-rockers like Sean and the Brandywines.

After taking a job with Columbia, Usher was handed a plum assignment: producing the Byrds.

His visionary and sympathetic work on their two critical LPs, 1967's *Younger than Yesterday* and 1968's *Notorious Byrd Brothers,* speaks for itself. He helped a crumbling band stick together long enough to record its two best albums.

Usher also produced the Byrds' next offering, the country-rock showpiece, *Sweetheart of the Rodeo.* In his capacity as a Columbia staff producer, he worked with the Peanut Butter Conspiracy, Chad and Jeremy, and Simon & Garfunkel.

Perhaps his greatest work as an artist came in collaboration with fellow L.A. writer/artist/producer Curt Boettcher. The two formed Sagittarius, whose *Present Tense* album is one of the great unheralded pop albums of the '60s. The album's single, "My World Fell Down," was a hit in most major markets during 1967.

Later, Usher would move into jingles. He would also found, with Boettcher and Keith Olsen (formerly a bass player with the Music Machine and later a successful producer), Together Records.

After a crazy decade, Usher pulled back from rock and into a more spiritual realm during the '70s. He reemerged, however, with a new album, *Sanctuary* (credited to Celestium), in 1983. He passed away in 1990.

4. QUINCY JONES

The man lionized as a pioneer in black entertainment, a hero to Oprah Winfrey and other African-American entertainment tastemakers, a leading light in jazz...yes, it's Quincy Jones, *who arranged...Leslie Gore's "It's My Party!"*

Yes, it was tough sailing for black producers back in the old days. But at the time he was arranging Leslie Gore's records, Jones was also a vice president of Mercury Records, Gore's label.

By the mid-'60s, he had become a favorite of movie producers for his excellent soundtrack music (his first assignment was *The Pawnbroker*), and he hasn't looked back.

Jones, who at last count has 26 Grammy awards on his shelf, produced two of the biggest records in history: Michael Jackson's *Thriller* and the single by USA for Africa, "We Are the World." His 1989 album, *Back on the Block,* was a showcase combining some of the great talents of American music (Ella Fitzgerald, Miles Davis, Dizzy Gillespie) with newer artists like Ice-T and Grandmaster Melle Mel.

In 2000, he put out *Q's Jook Joint,* another cross-cultural musicfest featuring performers as diverse as Bono, Gloria Estefan, Barry White, Herbie Hancock, Coolio, and Heavy D.

His record company, Qwest, boasts such diverse acts as New Order, Tevin Campbell, and Bebe and Cece Winans. Jones is also executive producer of the TV show, *Mad TV,* and his conglomerate publishes *Vibe* magazine.

That's a long way from "It's My Party."

5. SLY STONE

Sylvester Stewart is one of the first black men to produce white rockers (Tom Wilson, Bob Dylan's producer, may have been *the* first).

Stewart, a multi-instrumentalist and DJ while in college during the early '60s, met Tom Donahue (later responsible for creating free-form FM rock radio), who ran Autumn Records, a label that featured the Mojo Men, the Vejtables, and the Beau Brummels. Stewart was part of the production team that helped to record the Beau Brummels' national hits, the classics "Laugh, Laugh" and "Just a Little." He also was at the session for the Great Society's "Somebody to Love," a song that GS singer Grace Slick would take with her when she joined the Jefferson Airplane in 1966.

By 1967, Stewart wanted to make his own music. He recruited family members and friends—black, white, male, and female—changed his own name to Sly Stone, and formed Sly and the

James A. Newberry

Sylvester Stewart, better known as Sly Stone, made funk-rock music heard never before nor since.

Family Stone. It was a group like nobody had ever seen, or dared to form, at the time: a multiracial, multigendered band that jammed on soul and rock with jazzy abandon and plenty of psychedelic freaking out.

After several months of playing Bay Area clubs and schools, the group earned a contract with Columbia Records. Their first album, *A Whole New Thing,* certainly was, and the single, "Dance to the Music," dented the Top 10 in 1968.

In 1969–70, there was no more important American group than Sly and the Family Stone. Smash hits like "Everyday People," "Hot Fun in the Summertime," "Thank You Falettin Me Be Mice Elf Agin," and "Family Affair" established the Family as a band for all Americans.

Unfortunately, racial tensions, drugs, and mounting pressures affected Sly, and he began blowing gigs and playing sloppily. While the hits continued until 1974, the band was never quite the same following 1971's apocalyptic album, *There's a Riot Goin' On.*

6. NORMAN "HURRICANE" SMITH

An EMI staff engineer assigned to help George Martin record the Beatles, Smith—a jazz trumpeter, singer, and pianist as well as a knob-twiddler—enjoyed working with the Fabs until late 1965, when he became dissatisfied with the music being made for the *Rubber Soul* LP.

Smith went on to produce the first two Pink Floyd albums *(Piper at the Gates of Dawn* and *A Saucerful of Secrets)*, as well as the Pretty Things' underrated masterpiece, *S.F. Sorrow.* Many artists who worked with "Normal" praised his willingness to experiment in the studio.

Little more was heard from him, however, until late 1972, when Smith unexpectedly hit the charts—

as "Hurricane" Smith—with "Oh, Babe, What Would You Say?" The jazz novelty was his only American hit, reaching #3 on the charts.

Smith also played trumpet for the Liverpool band, The Teardrop Explodes, providing his distinctive soul/jazz work on their 1980 debut album, *Kilimanjaro*.

7. BUTCH VIG

Vig began his musical career as a drummer in two underrated Wisconsin pop bands, Spooner and Firetown, in the late '70s and early–mid '80s.

Two of his friends and fellow musicians, Duke Erikson and Steve Marker, would team up with Vig later to form Garbage with singer Shirley Manson, a heretofore obscure belter whose previous credit was singing with the failed band, Goodbye Mr. McKenzie.

But in the meantime, Vig apprenticed in recording studios, learning the engineering trade, and eventually got a chance to show his mettle. He recorded the *Siamese Dream* album for Chicago rockers Smashing Pumpkins, produced several records for the Sub Pop label, and met Nirvana, who had heard and enjoyed his various productions.

When Nirvana were signed to DGC for their first major-label project, the band asked that Vig sit in the producer's chair. Despite some initial grumbling from the record company, the band stood firm, and Vig provided the claustrophobic but effective production on Nirvana's gigantic 1991 *Nevermind* album.

Once Garbage got off the ground, with their own 1995 debut album spawning five hit singles around the world (including "Only Happy When It Rains"), Vig finally got his own taste of big-time rock stardom.

8. JOHN "JELLYBEAN" BENITEZ

Growing up in New York City, Benitez (born 1959) became involved in the city's dance music under-ground as a teenager. He hooked himself into the disco movement when it was at its peak, spinning records at Sanctuary, Studio 54, and Xenon.

Benitez became one of the first superstar DJs by taking his love for Latin music and his feel for what made a dance floor move and turning it into something all his own. Relentlessly pushing the boundaries of dance music, Benitez stayed a step ahead of trends and eventually became a taste-maker.

Moving into radio, Benitez experimented with remixing records. He soon began working for record companies and turned songs by artists as varied as Barbra Streisand, Ruben Blades, Pat Benatar, Marc Anthony, Madonna, Paul McCartney, and Michael Jackson into dance-floor hits. He also worked on remixing film music, scoring big with his versions of songs from the film *Flashdance.*

Benitez and singer Madonna Ciccone met at a club in the early '80s, and enjoyed a two-year relationship. He produced Maddy's early hits, "Borderline" and "Holiday," helping her get started on the road to superstardom.

But Benitez wasn't content to be behind the decks. He decided to record his own compositions, first releasing the *Wotupski* EP and an album, *Just Visiting this Planet.* His Latin hip-hop creation, "Sidewalk Talk," co-written by Madonna, was a Top 20 hit in late 1985.

Two years later, he scored his second Top 20 hit with "Who Found Who," a duet with singer Elisa Fiorillo. His second solo project was 1990's *Spilling the Beans,* another major hit.

In the last decade, Benitez has kept a full appointment book. He has composed music for motion pictures, written TV themes, and continued his lucrative remix work. Benitez has also worked to build up the Latin music community with his House of Latino Artists record company.

9. MITCH EASTER/DON DIXON

North Carolina rockers who started playing in the late '60s, Mitch Easter and Don Dixon were called in to produce an EP for the Georgia band, R.E.M., in 1982. The EP, *Chronic Town,* was produced at Easter's Drive-In Studio, outside his home in Winston-Salem, North Carolina.

Chronic Town was successful enough that IRS Records and R.E.M. asked the pair to co-produce their first two albums *(Murmur* and *Reckoning)* as well. This Easter and Dixon did with panache.

As their reputations grew, both Easter and Dixon produced other groups; Easter twirled the knobs for Game Theory and the Windbreakers, while Dixon produced Guadalcanal Diary and his wife, Marti Jones. R.E.M. chose to go to England and record their third album with Joe Boyd in 1985, making Easter and Dixon's moves into solo territory that much easier.

Dixon, who scored a major U.S. alternative hit in 1987 with "Praying Mantis," has released six original albums under his own name, while Easter's band, Let's Active, put out four quality records on IRS and played on major worldwide tours with bands like General Public, Echo and the Bunnymen, and R.E.M.

While neither has the high profile he did in the '80s, Easter and Dixon continue to produce and play their own music.

10. WILLIAM ORBIT

A techno pioneer who goes far outside the boundaries of his field, Orbit is an innovator who would have been a star in any era of recorded sound.

His first major assignment was co-producing Sting's "If You Love Someone, Set Them Free" single in 1985. He also remixed songs by artists from varying backgrounds: Stan Ridgway (of Wall of Voodoo), Belinda Carlisle, Doctor & The Medics, Prince, and Erasure.

However, Orbit also harbored his own dreams, fronting a three-piece band, Torch Song, before choosing the solo route in 1988. During the next decade or so, he would release several CDs, most of them on the periphery of dance music, and one classical CD, *Pieces in a Modern Style*.

Orbit's music—spacey, hypnotic, and experimental—crossed the frontiers of dance music and incorporated rock, classical, folk, and world elements.

His biggest success came with Madonna's 1998 *Ray of Light* album. Orbit's swirling, jarring, often disturbing, and frequently transcendent production was the trick that truly put Madonna back over the top after several near-misses. *Ray of Light,* featuring several songs co-written with Orbit, was the best of Madonna's career and reestablished her as a truly innovative artist.

Orbit continues to work with British singer Beth Orton occasionally. He also has produced hit recordings recently for Blur and All Saints and enjoyed a surprise British hit single at Christmas 1999 with a version of Samuel Barber's "Adagio for Strings."

Postscript

Ending this book with William Orbit, a dance and techno-influenced artist who has flirted with rock, pop, and classical music, was as much luck as it was by design. But the point is that the music keeps changing, and books can hardly keep up with the changes. That's where you come in.

If this book inspired you to think about your own categories, your own lists, or your own weird stories, or if you just read something you liked (or didn't like), we'd love to hear from you. Your ideas (with proper credit, of course) could end up in a second volume of *Rock & Roll's Most Wanted!*

Please address love letters, fan mail, gripes, and great ideas to:

Rock & Roll's Most Wanted
c/o Brasseys, Inc.
22841 Quicksilver Drive
Dulles, VA 20166-2012

And thanks again for reading. A book is nothing without someone to open it, and we all hope you enjoyed this one.

Index

About the Author

Stuart Shea's rock writing credits include contributions to the *Music Hound Guide to Lounge Music, Reactor Magazine,* and *New Scene.* A veteran rock musician who has contributed to the American Song-Poem Music Archives, Shea lives in Chicago.